ON THE EDGE
TEN ARCHITECTS
FROM CHINA

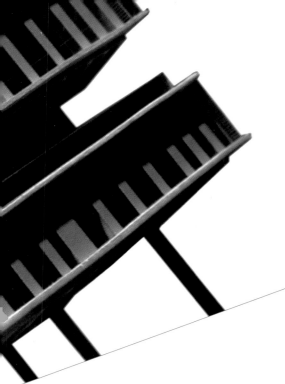

Edited by Ian Luna with Thomas Tsang / Introduction by Yung Ho Chang

ON THE EDGE
TEN ARCHITECTS
FROM CHINA

RIZZOLI
NEW YORK

OVERLEAF:

Model of Corporate Incubator,
Shongshan Lake, Dongguan City, Guandong Province
(Yung Ho Chang / Atelier Feichang Jianzhu, 2006 Completion)

First published in the United States of America
by Rizzoli International Publications, Inc.
300 Park Avenue South
New York, NY 10010
www.rizzoliusa.com

2006 2007 2008 2009 / 10 9 8 7 6 5 4 3 2 1

ISBN-13: 978-0-8478-2868-5
ISBN-10: 0-8478-2868-9
Library of Congress Control Number: 2006934610

Printed in China
Design coordination: Ian Luna & Eugene Lee

Edited by Ian Luna with Thomas Tsang / Introduction by Yung Ho Chang

ON THE EDGE
TEN ARCHITECTS
FROM CHINA

R

Throughout this publication, Chinese names follow the traditional order in which the family name precedes the given name. This is reversed in instances when the bearer's name follows Western custom or is otherwise a Western given name or secondary name.

ABOVE:

Songzhuan Art Center, Tongzhou District, Beijing
(Xu Tiantian / DnA Beijing, 2006)

Yung Ho Chang

A VERY BRIEF HISTORY OF MODERNITY

Make it very, very brief, if you like. In fact, this is an extremely short account of what can be hardly considered as history. As an architect rather than a scholar, I am sharing some of my observations and speculations on a few historic buildings and their architects in China, without the intention of delineating the full trajectory of the evolution of a modern architecture but to gain insights into the architecture *actualle* today.

A VERY BRIEF HISTORY

The beginning of Chinese modernity is commonly attributed to the First Opium War in 1840, when China was opened by European forces. Trade and communication with the world outside ensued. Subsequently, the May 4th Movement of 1919 introduced to China new ideas from the West—with democracy and science of long-lasting significance—and commenced in China the modern era in culture. It is obvious that Chinese modernity differs from the European in the critical role foreign influences played in its development. There was naturally the language problem— two in fact: (1) the translation of European concepts into Chinese; (2) the translation or transformation of classic Chinese into a modern one.

Thus, from 1910s onward, modern architecture in China emerged as a series of adoptions, adaptations, and translations of architecture from elsewhere as well as from the past. Since the majority of the first generation of architects active in China, both Chinese and foreign, were trained in the Beaux-Arts schools in the United States, they reproduced, sometimes faithfully, European Classicism and Art Deco and created in some other cases Chinese Classicism and Chinese Art Deco.

Meanwhile, European Modernism was made known in China by architects who studied in Europe but never gained much ground due to complex political, cultural, and professional reasons. What arouses my curiosity is not so much why it did not happen, but the few instances when it did happen and their implications.

LEFT TO RIGHT: *Peace Hotel, Beijing, 1953; Children's Hospital, Beijing, 1954.*[1]

MODERN AS STYLE

Peace Hotel, Beijing, 1953, by T. P. Yang (1901-1982)
This is one of the very first modern buildings in Beijing: an eight-story box in light gray plaster located in the central neighborhood of Wangfujing. While the building was certainly out of scale for a single-story context, Yang's effort in mediating the traditional urban fabric and preserving the existing trees on the site was well known, although his overall intent behind the design remains relatively opaque. The building became controversial and generated a heated debate on the issue of style—i.e. modern versus classical. Curiously, Yang was an architect who had a solid Beaux-Arts training at the University of Pennsylvania (he was a classmate of Louis Kahn and won the gold medal for his graduation project). And nowhere else did Yang show any interest in modern architecture. Either his modernist experiments were cut short by contemporary political pressure or he was trying out modernism as an alternative composition or style while applying classical principles. A similar exercise was accomplished in the past, to some extent: Yang's teacher at Penn, Paul Cret, approached modernism in the design of the Federal Reserve Board building in Washington in 1935 by stripping down classicism. While the ingenuity of Yang's work should not be overlooked, modernity, to his generation of Chinese architects, was merely a matter of style.

MODERN AS A SET OF PRINCIPLES, MODERN AS MODERN CHINESE

Children's Hospital, Beijing, 1954, by Lanhong (Leon) Hua (1912-)
When Hua designed the hospital on the west side of the city near the Temple of the Moon, not only did he employ an unmistakably modern architectural language—clean bar buildings of three to four stories (plus a semi-basement) with flat roofs—but also addressed the trademark issues of modernity: functionality, circulation, and space. While the complex distinguished itself from its classicist contemporaries, it also blended in with the surroundings. Its walls were built with the gray bricks that were typical of Beijing. A closer examination would have revealed Chinese decorative motifs and details at the corners of the cantilevered roofs, underneath the eaves, and on the balcony balustrades, often in the form of concrete relief. To the trained eye, the proportions of the concrete structure even resonated with the ancient Chinese timber frame. Hua went to France as a teenager, returned to China in 1951 after receiving an education and having a practice for a number of years, and brought back the European Modernism. Obviously, it was not enough nor appropriate for Hua to repeat what he learned, saw, and did in Europe, and he embarked immediately on a search for a modern architecture that might be Chinese. Cultural concerns aside, Hua intended to establish the modern concept of sanitation and health through design. However, as a victim of the Anti-Rightist Campaign, he was criticized in the mid 1950s for being a formalist. Consequently, modernism was superficially perceived in China as a set of fixed forms and aesthetics. The impact of such misreading of modernism, and to certain extent, of architecture in general, unfortunately lingers on.

MODERN AS IN MODERN THINKING

Lin's residence, Guangzhou, 1970s, by Lin Keming (1900-1999)
Lin, after returning from France in 1926 with an architectural diploma, built two houses for himself. The first one was more a stylistic take on European Modernism: the design sported a white, curving exterior but with divided spaces inside. The second one, built in the 1970s, was elevated from a small, sloped riverside lot and constructed with the typical material combination of the time: concrete and red clay bricks. The flat rooftop had to be used as a garden or a yard since the footprint of the house took almost the entire site. Inside, the public areas address the waterfront with the more private zones situated in the back. The building possesses no superior construction quality and is as crude as its neighbors, yet it shines with the wisdom of modernism and perhaps some of Le Corbusier's.

WHAT IS MODERNITY FOR CHINA?

A modernity from without:
Modernity = opening-up = influences from outside, mainly the West
The most important Western theory imported: Marxism
The notion of architecture as a body of knowledge as well as profession was also introduced from the West. In other words, architecture is modern in China.
As a result, the issue of cultural identity has existed from the very beginning of modernity.

A split modernity:
On one hand, a modernity that is nothing but ideology—Marxism and Socialism
On the other, a modernity voided of—and sometimes avoided of—substance:
Modernist style vs. modernity: as discussed above in architecture.
Modernization vs. modernity: technology, in the form of a flushable toilet, automobile, and air conditioner, is valued above science and other forms of modern thinking.

THE CURRENT ATTEMPT AT MODERNITY IN ARCHITECTURE

I have noticed the following peculiarities:
It reflects the two characteristics developed from history, specifically, the influence from the West and the simultaneous overdose and absence of ideology. Since China is re-embracing the market economy and is going through a major cultural transformation, the country today may be more open to Western ideas than the West itself and is more confused about -isms than ever before.

Within the old socialist system, some of the working class may have been provided basic housing but were often denied architecture. The architecture history books of modern China document civic monuments almost exclusively, but not buildings that matter in everyday life. Lin's House, for instance, does not appear in any publications. Although social welfare is presently in jeopardy, the range of building types that are now considered architecturally meaningful has been widened to include houses, multi-level housing, speculative real-estate schemes, retail, commercial facilities, and sometimes even very small buildings (such as tea rooms), evoking a democratizing tendency in architecture.

Reacting against the widespread use of Postmodernism—not Postmodernist philosophy but the pastiche of classicist aesthetics and contemporary conditions—and the visual chaos brought about by commercialism in the 1980s, Chinese architects have consciously turned to modernism for rescue. A principled, formal simplicity, and even austerity, has become a weapon in the battle against the eclecticism of consumption. However, minimalist design is quickly losing its fighting power as it is itself being consumed.

An effort has been made in architecture in recent years in China to go beyond style. Chinese architects are interested in space and tectonics in an unprecedented way. New materials are being explored and traditional materials used with unconventional methods. Yet the danger of sliding back into a style-conscious architecture is imminent, since some architects may have developed a dogmatic attitude towards a formal system of modernism, while others may be piling up the most-up-to-date gestures in projects in a move toward a kind of modern mannerism, since form-making has a higher priority than architects would be willing to admit.

This time around, there is even the opportunity to develop a modernity from within. In creative fields other than architecture—drama, fashion design, film, graphic design and the visual arts—the leading figures of the moment are rarely educated abroad, although some of them are very well informed about the global scene. Architecture is one of the few disciplines (music is another), in which returnees (including this author) are playing influential roles along with the home-grows. Translation still needs to be done, since the locally schooled architects are not confined by the definitions in the original languages and are free to interpret and invent.

The present-day Chinese situation is dynamic to the point of instability. New directions and concerns seem to surface frequently, such as a renewed interest in tradition that is not limited in form and imagery, and rewrites, rather than translates, the cultural text. The growing consciousness to social and environmental issues has as much of a chance of marrying design and ideology as it does in encouraging a greater divorce. Perhaps, as the title of this book indicates, contemporary Chinese architecture is very much on the edge of a freestanding wall, so it may fall on either side, or as a pluralist would predict, on both sides.

Where is modern or contemporary architecture in China heading? Maybe that is a question that can only be answered by a person with the privilege of time and space. As someone who is deeply caught in the action of making architecture in China, I have no time for either optimism or pessimism. I reflect, in order to move onto the next design challenge.

NOTES

[1] The images are from the *Illustrated Book of Beijing Architectures*, by the editors of Architectural Creation magazine (Beijing: China City Press, 2004), n. p.

Sze Tsung Leong

HISTORY IMAGES

PAGES 14-25:

Suzhou Jie, Daoxiangyuan, Haidian District, Beijing, 2004
Sze Tsung Leong
Chromogenic color print
72" x 87.5" (182.88 x 222.25 cm)

Datunxiang, Chaoyang District, Beijing, 2003
Sze Tsung Leong
Chromogenic color print
72" x 87.5" (182.88 x 222.25 cm)

Guomao Qiao, Chaoyang District, Beijing, 2004
Sze Tsung Leong
Chromogenic color print
72" x 87.5" (182.88 x 222.25 cm)

Chunshu, Xuanwu District, Beijing, 2004
Sze Tsung Leong
Chromogenic color print
72" x 87.5" (182.88 x 222.25 cm)

Xinjiekou, Xuanwu District, Nanjing, 2004
Sze Tsung Leong
Chromogenic color print
72" x 87.5" (182.88 x 222.25 cm)

Daochuan Long, Nan Shi, Huangpu District, Shanghai, 2004
Sze Tsung Leong
Chromogenic color print
72" x 87.5" (182.88 x 222.25 cm)

All images courtesy of the artist and Yossi Milo Gallery, New York, New York.

Ian Luna

STRUCTURAL CONTRADICTIONS

In an article that appeared in one of the lifestyle glossies that now proliferate in Beijing, Zhang Xin, one of the country's more visible property developers predicted in very certain terms that "just as China will have its own Picasso […] China's going to have its own Le Corbusier."[1]

She wasn't about to name names, but the statement concluded a far-ranging exposition on the current architectural state of play in China, and the lead up to her exclamation provides an instructive look at the rhetorics of a nascent discourse. A Hong Kong resident expatriated to England and now firmly planted in the Chinese capital, Zhang's career as architectural benefactor began with a number of important large-scale works in and around the city, including a number of mid-rise tower blocks within the new Guomao central business district east of Beijing's imperial axis. At the helm of SOHO China, the company she founded with husband Pan Shiyi, she obtained considerable fame and influence outside China especially after the completion of eleven model villas under the shadow of the Badaling Great Wall in 2002. The houses in this modern commune were notable as much for their robust experiment as for Zhang's insistence on drafting only Asian designers for each manse, with many of the indigenous participants born in Mainland China.

Indeed, much of Zhang's reputation in the West presumes an aggressive promotion of local talent. Zhang herself is quick to point out her collaborations with a number of Beijing standbys, and that crucially, she "was the very first client of Yung Ho Chang,"[2] the figure most associated with the imminence of the new architecture. Which isn't to say that SOHO China has any misgivings about spreading the wealth to non-Chinese practices. It is precisely her manifest role in opening up China to North American, European, Japanese and Australian star-shops that has made her company something of a lightning rod for nationalists among the chattering classes. Frequently, the brand-new developer class has been caricatured as lukewarm mentors to the country's native sons and daughters, accused of passing them over to work with foreigners at the first opportunity.

As if in confirmation, the only quotes gathered from early SOHO China collaborators Cui Kai and Zhu Xiaodi are one-liners in a sidebar to the Zhang interview, where the architects lament that either "many developers know nothing about domestic architects" or that "a lot of the projects invite only foreign firms to bid, or require us to work with foreign firms in order to bid […] as if we in China have nothing to offer." To establishment critics, the stakes are much higher than primacy in commissions. Wu Liangyong, the doyen of the architectural old guard at Tsinghua Univerisity, who had spent the better part of the 1990s developing nostalgic forms of multi-level housing in old Beijing,[3] hints at a great game for the soul of Chinese cities. A participant in the expansion of Tian'anmen Square to its present size, he expresses a profound discomfort with all this openness and risk-taking. Nevermind that the ancient, densely inhabited cores of Beijing and Shanghai now under wholesale obliteration were only "preserved" for much of the communist era by poverty and neglect rather than force of will,[4] Wu notes that cities in China have shortchanged their patrimony to "become 'experimental sites' for both noted foreign architects and some second- and third-level ones."[5]

Less temperate views on the qualitative direction of design and urbanization abound in print. And the ease of imputing the spectacles of ugliness blighting Chinese cities at the feet of invited outsiders point to one of the great paradoxes of Chinese history: the attraction to and suspicion of foreigners. The will to summon the old saw of Western and Japanese colonialism in Asia, and the use of overheated language ("carving up," "neo-imperialist," "Concessions") migrate easily from online bulletin boards to academia. Uttered chiefly for internal consumption, these provocative lexical choices, far from acquiring any semantic drift since the high tide of the Mao years, have in fact maintained their potency. This rubric is particularly evident in a political context where the state occasionally scripts "simultaneous popular expressions" against the usual foreign targets to deflect attention from the very real unrest in the countryside.

In this charged setting, Zhang's contradictory response to the opprobrium reflects the complex role of nationalism in the civic and intellectual life of the country. Signaling some exasperation with this debate, she professes to ignore her detractors, but forwards a syllogism that emphasizes the value of unfettered experiment, recalls the diverse geographic origin of innovative ideas and repudiates the dangerous naivety of us-against-them. She then tersely declares that there is "no such thing as nationalism for Chinese architecture. One should face it instead of saying 'We're Chinese; we only want to use Chinese.' The world has changed. We don't live in a place where people live in courtyards and wear the long ponytails worn by men during the Qing Dynasty! [lit., *chang bian zi*]." She goes on however to describe the role of technology in creating a "moment" for contemporary Chinese architecture, and that in the future SOHO China will create an award to promote the work of Chinese architects, with criteria encouraging the use of Chinese culture."[6] She dismisses Wu Liangyong's cautionary polemic by way of a somewhat ecumenical non-conclusion: "it is easy to be critical and say things, but if thousands of people are putting their life savings into something, there is reasonable justification for it. That is the beauty of a developer's project: everything is for sale."

Zhang's pronouncements make for good copy in a megalopolis caught up in a delirium of building and engineering, which saw the total volume of new construction in Beijing—of all types, completed or under way through 2006—equal to the land area of two Manhattans. And in the heady climate anticipating the 2008 Summer Games, the Le Corbusier prophecy intimates a broader discussion on the fundamental, and highly visible roles played by architects and planners in the sustainable development of China, the argument over national identity, and the future of foreign tuition in the transformation of urban space.[7]

Standing explicitly to the side of the dominant discourses on China in the West, this aspirational conversation about the notional value of an indigenous architectural "genius" and the real value of a contemporary, even critical architectural idiom can only be understood, and thus enumerated within the context of a much larger plot. In one of the more delicious ironies of China's outrageous fortunes, two generations of architects, many the alumni of a collectivized and intellectually isolated trade for whom the very idea of private individual practice was anathema as late as two decades ago, are now poised to achieve the fullness of global notoriety. The emergence of an avant-garde, the accelerated maturation of indigenous models for architectural practice, and the present formal diversity in architectural expression grew out of a unique set of historical conditions, and is bound intimately with the last three decades of Chinese revolutionary politics and the economic policies at the core of all cultural production.

SEEKING TRUTH FROM FACTS

In the wake of the country's accession to the World Trade Organization and the awarding of the Beijing Olympiad, then paramount leader Jiang Zemin summed up China's terms for a continued, muscular engagement with 21st-century globalization. Called the Three Represents and composed in the arcane tongue of high officialdom, Jiang elevated it to doctrine to the assembled deputies at 16th National Congress of the Communist Party of China (CPC) in the fall of 2002:

"The theme of the congress is to hold high the great banner of Deng Xiaoping Theory, fully act on the important thought of Three Represents, carry forward our cause into the future, keep pace with the times, build a well-off society in an all-round way, speed up socialist modernization and work hard to create a new situation in building socialism with Chinese characteristics. [...] The historical experience gained by the Party since its founding can be summarized as follows: Our Party must always represent the development trend of China's advanced productive forces (1), the orientation of China's advanced culture (2) and the fundamental interests of the overwhelming majority of the Chinese people (3). They are the inexorable requirements for maintaining and developing socialism and the logical conclusion our Party has reached through hard exploration and great practice."[8]

Number One of the Three Represents is often deciphered as an official acknowledgment of the contribution of "advanced productive forces"—the new entrepreneurial classes—in the rise of China, and affords a provocative rationale for their induction among the party faithful. Represent Number Two reaffirms a conception of Chinese Marxism as a "developing science" with the natural capacity and mutability to realize the "present needs of modernization, the world and the future."[9]

In emancipating capitalist agency, the Three Represents merely scribes an evolutionary stage within a long ideological continuum. The deductive processes that recast the base alloy of counterrevolutionary ideas into the shining gold of contemporary orthodoxy have clearly been at work for some time, and the resulting framework, "Deng Xiaoping Theory,"[10] is shorthand for a program of nearly three decades of economic liberalization that began with the introduction of free market forces in 1978. Its objective was to foster "Socialism with Chinese Characteristics," an eminently flexible developmental model[11] that while it increasingly acquires unmistakable neoliberal traits, resolutely affirms the primacy of the state in determining the direction and extent of change, and the limits of social and political enfranchisement.

The interoperable concepts of Deng Xiaoping Thought and Socialism with Chinese Characteristics trace their origins to the venomous political climate immediately before and after the deaths of Zhou Enlai and Mao Zedong in 1976. The cycles of renunciation, repudiation and rehabilitation that reached their cruel perigee during the Cultural Revolution nourished a cadre well suited to ideological flexibility and weary of violent struggles for succession. Pressed between the opposite poles of a radical mass movement and a conservative retrenchment, proponents of a third way united around Deng Xiaoping. Purged by Mao for his economic pragmatism, reeducated in a tractor factory, restored by the ailing Zhou, and then purged again by the Gang of Four, Deng finally assumed the practical (if never the titular) chairmanship of the Party by the early 1980s.

The principal beneficiary of Zhou's patronage, Deng was also the inheritor of a four-point national agenda, which, once married with an increasing rapprochement and material exchange with the West, was to form the basis of "reform and opening." Dubbed as the Four Modernizations, which

Zhou outlined as early as 1964, it called for the modernization of agriculture, industry, national defense, and science and technology by end of the century. Later codified into Deng Xiaoping Thought, the opening gambit of this reform program emphasized Modernizations Two and Four—arguably at the expense, in absolute terms, of Modernization One—and set in motion a series of events that ultimately transformed a sclerotic command economy into an export-oriented market system within a generation. Maintaining that the Chinese economy was in the teething stages of socialism, Deng and his ascendant clique effectively reset the clock and put forward a theoretical précis for economic experimentation. Still stretched over the organizational framework of successive five-year plans, the practical application of the Four Modernizations were assigned more modest goals, and contrasted markedly with the calamitous mass mobilization programs of the Mao era. A period of readjustment, from 1977 through the early eighties, saw growth year-on-year—unlike the early to mid-seventies, when political instability and natural disasters begat general declines in agricultural and industrial output.

INSTANT CHINA

The reformers sought above all to ease Marxist controls over economic policy by emulating aspects of advanced capitalist countries as they rejected out of hand an incendiary suggestion by the activist Wei Jingsheng for a "Fifth Modernization" in the form of greater political and intellectual pluralism. Promptly sending its author to the gulag in 1979, the Deng line then set about relaxing government controls and ramping up the role of market mechanisms in the administration of both the agrarian and manufacturing sectors. In contrast to comparable market socialist initiatives elsewhere, Beijing discouraged a top-down approach, and measures were instead incubated in villages and towns before they were visited on whole provinces. In the countryside, a policy was implemented that for the first time favored material inducements over coercion as a means of increasing productivity. As the last of the People's Communes were dismantled, a contract responsibility scheme was introduced in 1980 whereby peasants could work the land for profit and were subsequently enabled to sell surplus yield at market-determined prices. This had the salutary effect of stabilizing agricultural production, and the consequent rises in the standard of living positively affected the ability of the state to absorb the political costs of more reform. Incipient forms of individual enterprise were encouraged in cities, as light industry and a formal service sector were developed in tandem as a counterweight to the underperforming state-owned enterprises (SOEs) that made up the manufacturing sector, where a new labor contract system eventually put an end to the "iron ricebowl" of lifelong employment.[12]

The second stage in "reform and opening" would see a decisive shift of capital assets from agriculture and state-subsidized industry to foreign trade. This transition was to first occur in controlled trials, and in 1979, Special Economic Zones (SEZs) were inaugurated to serve as its laboratories. Four coastal towns on the South China Sea—Shenzhen, Zhuhai, Xiamen and Shantou—were selected chiefly for their proximity to the "advanced commercial societies" of Taiwan and Hong Kong. The SEZs benefited immediately from procedural easements that granted individuals license to negotiate directly with foreign companies, permitting the country to take in foreign capital, legalize foreign investment, organize a workable banking system and acquire foreign know-how. The factories, imported experts, container ships, shopping malls and skyscrapers followed in short order.

Taken together, these four original SEZs—and the addition of fourteen other cities by 1984—would coalesce and mutate into a China that by century's end was arguably the preeminent sociological phenomenon of the age. Scarcely recognizable to the party's founding generation these instant cities multiplied at rates that continue to astound ethnographers and urban historians, mirroring the growth of a national economy that had been in absolute decline since the 18th century. Growing tenfold since 1978, the GDP climbed an ever-upward trajectory, ascending to the world's seventh largest in 2004—and handily leapfrogged over Italy, France and Britain to become its fourth in 2005.[13]

THE OWNERSHIP NON-OWNERSHIP SOCIETY

But for all the statistical hyperbole often employed to quantify its fruits, the seismic changes brought about by a conscious policy of market liberalization belie less than deliberate causes, follow less than inexorable courses, and body forth innumerable structural and lived contradictions. China's makeover into the "workshop of the world" enabled the transition of hundreds of millions from poverty to the middle classes in the greatest economic migration in history. But in a country that during much of the Mao era saw the world's smallest variation in absolute and mean incomes, the disparity between rural and urban wages is now one of the most pronounced in the world.

Inevitably, the manufacturing and services bonanza in the coastal cities severely outpaced the rate of growth in the rural interior, so much so that by 2005, agriculture—ostensibly still the primary industry—accounted for a little more than a tenth of the national income. Inversely, the total volume of imports and exports, which had never been more than a tenth of the GDP in the Mao era, ballooned to two-thirds. For a Party that idealized the virtues of an agrarian society much more ruthlessly than Soviet communism, the farmers were clearly losing out, with nearly eight out of ten rural Chinese subsisting on less than $1,500 a year, barely a third of the nominal per capita GDP of city dwellers.[14] Reforms in the cities also availed urban Chinese of full property rights by the turn of the century, while the mass of the peasantry remain bound to a system of ownership that bars individual households from assuming title to land.

The accelerating disparity between rural and urban incomes soon had millions of surplus agricultural laborers running pell-mell into the coastal areas. While many formed the backbone of the largely migrant labor force in the SEZs, the remainder were reduced to marginal avocations—or else left to the depredations of transpacific people-smugglers, who operate with impunity in the southeastern provinces. Fraught with consequences that have yet to run their course, this mass exodus triggered the collapse of the system of residency permits that the state employed for decades as a means of retarding the geographic and social mobility of its mostly rural citizens.[15]

Without proper documents and competing with the resident poor in their adopted cities, this "floating population" of aliens, numbering as much as two hundred million,[16] often relocated to regions that were themselves in great social upheaval. Concentrated in the larger cities, the country's heavy industry was locked in an iron ring of SOEs that stubbornly resisted change. Long moribund, the public sector had by the early 1990s become a festering sore, hemorrhaging money even as it poached hard-earned cash from the agricultural sector to stay afloat. The urgent goal of forcibly returning these enterprises "running in the red to profitability" by decade's end however failed to appreciate the extent to which the ensuing shock therapy would devastate urban communities.[17] The effects proved particularly acute in the rust belt of the east and northeast, where widespread factory closures forced tens of millions of people out of work.

Amplifying this demographic catastrophe, old myths about public virtue—especially the one about government promoting the common interest over that of the individual's—had eroded completely. Bureaucratic lassitude and corruption from the village committee level on up rose exponentially with the GDP. The many resentments bred by endemic graft are now seen as grave threats to the state itself and often combine with other longstanding political grievances to erupt in open unrest. Over 87,000 "public-order disturbances" were logged in 2005, up from 10,000 a decade ago. Blamed variously on "'bad elements,' 'thuggish idlers,' 'individuals with ulterior motives,' even 'agents of overseas anti-China forces'"[18] these incidents were almost always rooted in rising inequity.

Social cohesion is then almost entirely dependent on the capacity of the state to sustain a level of growth that can weather a tolerable degree of restiveness. In the China of market socialism, politics is reducible to a form of scientific management, and acts of repression—still implemented by public security organs with exaggerated severity—are merely evidence of a normative approach to maintaining stability. But words often precede blunt-force trauma. In concert with the current "Strike Hard" anticorruption campaign, President Hu Jintao's contribution to the canon of party aphorisms, the "8 Do's and 8 Don'ts," sternly admonishes the people to uphold civic harmony and combat hedonism by not making "selfish gains to the detriment of others," or "wallowing in luxuries and pleasures."[19]

The sheer accretion of commercial and residential floor space in China's cities can then be interpreted as the physical monument to the success of Deng Xiaoping Thought, the prosperity behind it a reward to the urban classes for upholding their obligations to a social contract that was strained to the breaking point in 1989. The city in post-Deng China is at once an irrepressible, even radical site for economic interaction and a confining place where the interpretative threshold of these activities is plainly marked out. Surveillance and self-policing are vital rudiments to this conception of urban space, and like most forms of public expression, improper variation is inhibited at the outset.

THE ARCHITECTURE OF OPPORTUNITY

The paths to a contemporary Chinese architecture and individual private practice illustrate the complexities of a "socialism advancing with the times," which attempts to reconcile the purest forms of free market enterprise with wide-ranging state controls. Prior to the liberalizations of the present era, indigenous architectural production within the People's Republic was the exclusive province of state-run design institutes, which were spiritually derived from Soviet antecedents. In a manner similar to the privatization of manufacturing, many of these guilds were broken up and left to the vagaries of the market. Their dissolution would in time lead to a round of mergers, signifying the ability of the more profitable institutes to find new impetus in an incredibly generous market for design services. The Beijing Institute of Architectural Design—responsible for perpetrating the two monumental buildings flanking Tian'anmen Square, the Great Hall of the People and the Museum of Chinese Revolution—presently has a staff of over 400 architects and 500 engineers minus support staff, dwarfing most comparable Western shops in size and clientele.[20]

Fortunately, the more talented progeny of these institutes chose to permanently opt out of the groupmind. Free to strike out on their own, the constituents of this embryonic avant-garde received invaluable apprenticeships either outside the country, or internally, with the many foreign practices that were tasked by some of the more enlightened of the pioneering real-estate developers in the SEZs to bridge the chasm between their towering ambitions and the inadequacies of the local skill set.

It is no accident that part of this professional reeducation should occur in the pilot SEZs. Fundamental to the theory behind the zones is the role of technology transfer in the implementation of the national project. Accordingly, the three chief ordinances that governed Sino-foreign trade, The Law of the People's Republic of China on Chinese-Foreign Equity Joint Ventures, the Law on Chinese-Foreign Contractual Joint Ventures and the Law on Wholly Foreign-Owned Enterprises stipulate the developmental rationale with some granularity: "in order to expand economic cooperation and technological exchange with foreign countries and to promote development of the Chinese national economy."[21]

These guiding principles oversaw the incipient architectural exchanges of the 1980s and 1990s, and had a profound effect on indigenous practice. In a context where all economic activities are permitted to flourish insofar as they advance national conveniences, architecture and planning occupy a position distinct from other expressive forms of cultural production. Prized as agents of both physical transformation and psychological uplift, architecture and its allied trades are formally described as tertiary services that add value to manufacturing and construction enterprises. The premise that all work is political work is as yet unreconstructed and denies—at least in an official sense—a conception of architecture as an independently legible field of endeavor.

SINOFICATION

Foreign architectural firms, heralded by design practices from neighboring Asian countries, were instrumental in furnishing the critical infrastructure for the SEZs. Their introduction mimicked the process whereby other segments of the diversifying economy imported technocrats to jump-start productivity. The majority of non-Chinese firms presently engaged in the country will continue to play an important but ultimately transitional role in the transfer of technology. The present demand for Western creativity and tutelage exists within the same order that imposes protectionist constraints on the activity of its generative agents. These barriers range from broad market exclusions to practical ordinances that almost always favor rapid project turnaround over higher construction quality. China's entry into the WTO has mitigated somewhat the more onerous of these measures, but for a time, wholly foreign-owned practices were limited to projects completely funded by foreign capital, or else to those "which Chinese construction enterprises could not undertake independently due to technical difficulties."[22] Whereas it is not always expressly avowed, the legal conveyances are in place to limit foreign participation, in order that the upper hand in Sino-foreign collaborations can shift irresistibly to indigenous firms over time.

The new and improved Chinese architect is thus the product of a necessary juncture between East and West, an economic agent with a meaningful level of practical autonomy, empowered by the unwieldy role nationalism often plays in the narrative of emerging markets. For all its perils, the tonic of a resurgent pan-Chinese identity remains the only force in the nation capable of supplanting the flagging persuasive appeal of Mao Zedong Thought and its intellectual heirs. The significant achievements of the past decade have since shown that appeals to national identity can engender critical responses. An expansive notion of what it means to be Chinese also ensures that that the large Chinese diaspora in the West will continue to be a bridge, transmitting ideas and talent long after much of the intended Sinofication of the trade condenses the presence of foreign firms to a reduced orbit of star-shops and international design personalities.

Hailing from the largest diasporic community reincorporated thus far (if only administratively) into the People's Republic, the Hong Kong architect Rocco Yim assumes a philosophical line on the pan-Chinese identity and its whys and wherefores:

"What does it mean being Chinese in the making of architecture? What is expected of a Chinese person in his work? Will 'Chinese-ness' come about by the architect being Chinese, or by the context being Chinese, or both, or neither? Is 'Chinese-ness' genuinely discernable, a quality that can be consciously pursued? Or is it something that comes from within, a subtle reflection of personality, conditioned by ancestral mentality and taste, and therefore incidental rather than intentional? But is not the value ultimately more in the asking?"[23]

Yim wisely avoids the easy irony of ending this line of inquiry on a hypothetical question:

"We should not feel obliged—being Chinese or being an architect designing in China—to be different. Yet on the other hand we recognize there is a need to fulfill a different mission and respond to a different set of criteria."[24]

He sheds no insight on the hypothetical Le Corbusier of his repeat client, Zhang Yin, but he does not deny the reality of nationalism and its manifold demands. Chinese-ness is neither good nor bad, but like the weather, just is. With change as the engine, contemporary Chinese architecture exists in a state of constant becoming, and much like China itself, it is in this variability, volatility and interpretative complexity that much of its meaning resides.

[1] Daragh Moller, "China's going to have its own Le Corbusier: Zhang Xin/ SOHO: Thinking Tomorrow," *Beijing This Month*, September 2004, issue 130, n.p. The publication was sponsored by the Information Office of the Beijing Municipal Government.

[2] Ibid.

[3] Wu Liangyong, *Rehabilitating the Old City of Beijing: A Project in the Ju'Er Hutong Neighborhood* (Vancouver: University of British Columbia Press, 2000), pp. 66, 182.

[4] Sze-Tsung Leong, *History Images* (Göttingen, Germany: Steidl, 2006), pp. 138-141.

[5] Daragh Moller, "China's going to have its own Le Corbusier": Zhang Xin/SOHO: Thinking Tomorrow," *Beijing This Month*, September 2004, issue 130, n.p.

[6] Ibid., passim. "Every great architecture embodies a moment, and the character of that moment. To me, ours is technology."

[7] According to market data released in the fall of 2005 by the United States Commercial Service, a division of the Department of Commerce, the total value of architecture, construction and engineering services in China is estimated at $315 billion. "The Architecture, Construction and Engineering (ACE) Services in China," The United States Commercial Service, September 25, 2005, p. 1. Figures from the end of 2001 cited by the same agency in an earlier report suggest the proportion of the current labor force engaged in some form of building work: "There were 36.69 million people working in the construction industry, and there are 65,671 architecture, construction and engineering companies in China."

[8] Excerpted from the full text of Jiang Zemin's Report at the 16th National Congress of the Chinese Communist Party in Beijing, First Session, November 8, 2002.

[9] "[We] must clearly understand that Marxism is a developing science...new experience and understanding gained from practice must be constantly assimilated and used to enrich and develop Marxism." Extracted from the white paper "On the Three Represents: First expositions of the important thought of Three Represents." International Department of Central Committee of the CPC, 2003, n.p.

[10] Or more appropriately, Deng Xiaoping Thought, for within Maoist ideology, thoughts assume greater mass than theories.

[11] Chinese market socialism is sometimes idealized as a neo-Confucian developmental model. Peter L. Berger and Michael Hsiao, eds., *In Search of an East Asian Developmental Model* (New Brunswick, NJ: 1988). A critique on the applicability of the model outside China is offered by Martin Hart-Landsberg and Paul Burkett, *China & Socialism: Market Reforms and Class Struggle* (New York: Monthly Review Press, 2005)

[12] Deng Yuan Hsu and Pao-yu Ching, "Labor Reform: Mao vs. Liu-Deng," in Jose Maria Sison and Stefan Engel, eds., *Mao Zedong Thought Lives: Essays in Commemoration of Mao's Centennial* (Utrecht: Center for Social Studies, 1995 & Essen, Germany: Verlag Neuer Weg, 1995.), pp. 188-213.

[13] China ended 2005 with a nominal GDP of over $2.23 trillion, behind only Germany, Japan and the United States. "China's economy grew by 9.9% in 2005," *China People's Daily (Renmin Ribao)*, January 26, 2006, n.p.

[14] Ibid. The nominal per capita GDP in 2005 was $1,700. Any attempt to stem rural migration—even with projections that sees the aggregate urban population growing by no more than four percentage points, (from about 41 to 45) percent of the total population between 2005 and 2010—cannot hope to keep up with the rate mean incomes are doubling and tripling in the cities. Gui-Ying Cao et al., *Interim Report (IR-03-042) on Regional Population Projections for China* (Laxenburg, Austria: International Institute for Applied Systems Analysis, December 2003), pp. 4-5.

[15] The rural population, far from declining, grows apace despite rapid urbanization: "The urban population occupied 42.99% of the overall population; the rural population occupied 57.01% of the overall population. As compared with that in the 5th National Population Census [begun in 2000], the proportion of rural population to overall population was up by 6.77 percentage points." Communiqué on Major Data of 1% National Population Sample Survey in 2005, National Bureau of Statistics of China, March 16, 2006.

[16] Ibid. Official figures peg the "floating population" at 147.35 million in 2005. These numbers exclude significant illegal migration into the Hong Kong Special Administrative Region (SAR).

[17] Cited from "Major objectives set by 15th CPC Congress achieved," *China People's Daily (Renmin Ribao)*, November 07, 2002, n.p.; "Initial success achieved in State-owned economic restructuring," *China People's Daily (Renmin Ribao)*, November 16, 2004, n.p.

[18] Lianjiang Li, "Divide and Rule: Beijing Fears the Power of an Organized Citizenry," *Time Magazine Asia*, March 13, 2006; "China handles 87,000 public order disturbance cases," Xinhua News Agency, Jan 20, 2006.

[19] Also known as the "8 Honors and 8 Disgraces," these were first enumerated when Hu was the chief ideologue of the Party Central Committee in the 1990s, and assumed the heft of theory in a nationwide campaign launched in March 2006. "New Moral Yardstick: 8 Honors, 8 Disgraces," Xinhua News Agency, April 5, 2006."

[20] As of this writing, the sixty largest ACE (architectural, construction, engineering) firms are "restructured" institutes.

[21] From Article 1 of The Law of the People's Republic of China on Wholly Foreign-Owned Enterprises. The Law of the People's Republic of China on Chinese-Foreign Equity Joint Ventures was adopted and promulgated on July 1,1979, and revised in April 1990. The Law of the People's Republic of China on Chinese-Foreign Contractual Joint Ventures was adopted and promulgated on April 13,1988. The Law of the People's Republic of China on Wholly Foreign-Owned Enterprises was adopted and promulgated on April 12,1986.

[22] "The Architecture, Construction and Engineering (ACE) Services in China," The United States Commercial Service, September 25, 2005, pp. 4-6.

[23] Rocco Yim, Laurent Gutiérrez, Valérie Portefaix et al., *Being Chinese In Architecture: Recent Works in China by Rocco Design* (Hong Kong: MCCM, 2004), p. 2.

[24] Ibid., pp. 12-13.

SELECTED PROJECTS

TONG MING / TM STUDIO

Demonstrating a profound understanding of the nature and historical development of urbanization in China, TM Studio—established in Shanghai by Tong Ming in 1998—seeks to "integrate such increasingly disconnected phenomena as past and present, imagination and reality, events and environment." In practice, the studio's philosophical approach draws particular force from Tong's thorough understanding of the unique material condition of the cities of the Yangtze River Basin. His current commercial and institutional work in the *über*-historic cities of Suzhou and Nanjing exhibit all the markers of an incipient critical regionalism.

Tong Ming was born in 1968. In 1990 and 1993, respectively, he received his bachelors and masters degrees in architecture from Southeast University in Nanjing China, and in 1999, his Ph.D. in Urban Planning from Tongji University in Shanghai. Since that time, Ming has taught at the College of Architecture and Urban Planning in Shanghai as an associate professor of urban planning.

In addition to Dong's House Restaurant, recent representative works of TM Studio include Wenzheng College of Suzhou University, Suzhou (design completed in 2005), and theInternational Club in Nanjing (completed in 2005), both in Jiangsu Province.

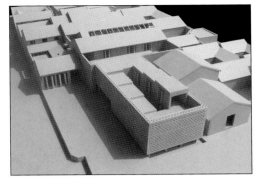

LEFT TO RIGHT: *Model view of master plan looking west; view looking south.*

TM Studio / Tong Ming with Chen Ming
Suzhou, Anhui Province, 2004

DONG'S HOUSE RESTAURANT

Described with not a little exaggeration by Marco Polo in his *Travels* as a city of "six thousand bridges, all of stone, and so lofty that a galley, or even two galleys at once, could pass underneath one of them," Suzhou remains one of the best preserved of China's ancient cities, its surfeit of historic sites linked by a grid of picturesque waterways diverted from the Grand Canal. Occupying a central location in the Yangtze basin between Shanghai and the great Tai Lake, the trickle of foreign tourists to Suzhou has grown appreciably since the glory days of Kublai Khan and his excitable Venetian guest.

Much of the economic activity Polo observed is also still evident some eight centuries on: "they possess silk in great quantities, from which they make gold brocade and other stuffs, and they live by their manufactures and trade." Motorola, Matsushita, Philips and a hundred other agents of globalization that set up shop in the National Hi-Tech Park west of Suzhou proper have long over-taken the silkworm as the primary engine of hard currency, and the shift in the mode of production has gone some way in rehabilitating the crumbling downtown and its famous canals into a nostalgic playground for the emerging leisure class. The six main canals that travel east to west intersect the six north to south canals at right angles, and are in turn traversed by some two hundred bridges of varying widths. The gentrifying Ping Jiang neighborhood typifies the unique urban character of the old quarter, with its serried ranks of residential and small industrial structures addressing the water "street."

Prefaced by a paved square along one of the north-south channels, Dong's House Restaurant sits on the rectangular footprint of a former factory, and is the focus of a master plan initiated by the municipality to transform a small number of surrounding buildings into a magnet for development. While the shell and spatial configuration of the residential structures to the south of the project area were preserved to maintain historic continuity, this 19,400-square-foot (1,800 m²) café and restaurant was specifically conceived as a contemporary amenity among the restored buildings. Its austere principal facade, clad in hollow bricks coursed on their side, is a screen that provides views of the waterfront during the day, and a lantern announcing the revival of the neighborhood at night. But the restaurant's most modern gesture takes the form of a spiraling floor that rises in 15-inch (40 cm) increments to achieve the three-story height of the building, terminating into a terraced roof. The restaurant functions evoke the spatial qualities of traditional teahouses organized around a courtyard, with operable wooden shutters that expand to afford patrons a greater sense of privacy, or else fold to the side to permit views across the width of the building.

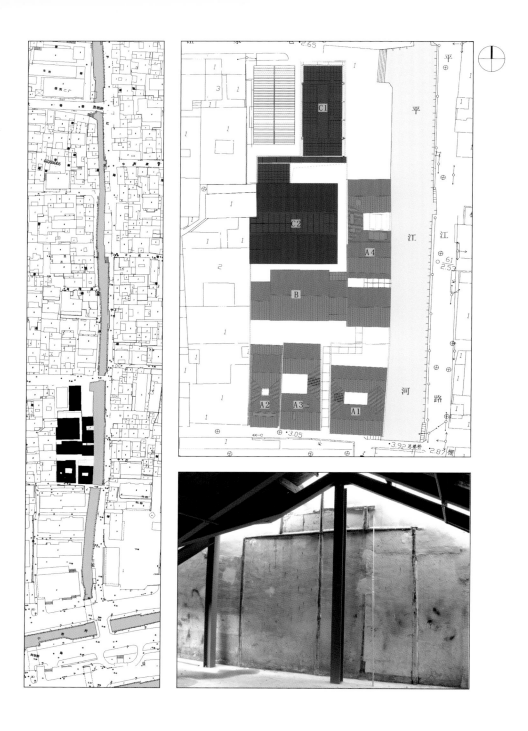

CLOCKWISE FROM LOWER LEFT: *Neighborhood map; master plan with restaurant and restored courtyard residences; view of restored residential interior with steel structure in place of traditional wood supports.*

44

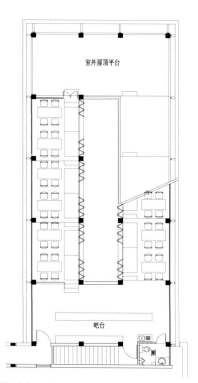

室外屋顶平台

吧台

Third floor plan

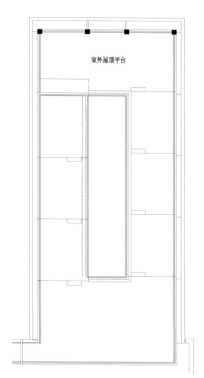

室外屋顶平台

Roof plan

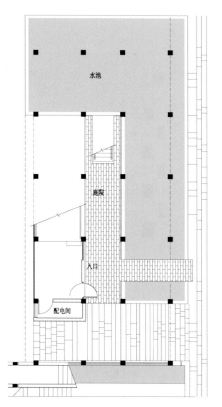

水池

庭院

入口

配电间

Ground floor plan

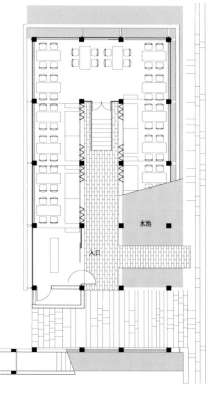

水池

入口

Second floor plan

LIU JIAKUN / JIAKUN ARCHITECTS

Based out of Sichuan Province, Jiakun Architects negotiates a professional orbit defined by central and southwestern China's three largest cities—Chengdu, Changsha and Chongqing—but has of late seen an expansion to sites in the north and east of the country. Led by the architect and writer Liu Jiakun, the work of the firm was described variously at landmark expositions on modern Chinese architecture at the Centre Pompidou in Paris (Alors, La Chine?, 2003) and at the Netherlands Architecture Institute in Rotterdam (China Contemporary, 2006) as a "hybrid of the modern tradition" and Chinese precedent.

In practice this conception of the firm's work has less to do with appropriating and pressing native forms to new service. It is rather a considered accommodation of the material specificity of a given geographic boundary—and more importantly, working within the limitations of local building trades to create economical, but well-wrought and indisputably modern interventions. This careful balancing act resulted in a number of successful outings, including the much-lauded Luyeyuan Stone Sculpture Museum in Chengdu, Sichuan Province (2001), and the more recent Teaching Building for the Sculpture Department of the Sichuan Fine Arts Institute in the provincial-level municipality of Chongqing (2004). Liu's most recent constructions include a delicate sequence of elevated steel-and-glass teahouses for the Architectural Park that Ai Weiwei planned in Jinhua, Zhejiang Province (2006).

Liu Jiakun was born in Chengdu in 1956 and graduated from Department of Architecture of Chongqing Institute of Architecture and Engineering in 1982. In 1999, he established Jiakun Architects—formally Jiakun Architect & Associates—and specializes in architecture, interior and landscape design.

Jiakun Architects / Liu Jiakun with Wang Lun
Chengdu, Sichuan Province, 2001

LUYEYUAN
STONE SCULPTURE MUSEUM

Enlisted to design a 9,700-square-foot (900 m²) museum for religious statuary dating back some two thousand years, Liu Jiakun utilized the natural features of the site and its relative isolation to create a meditative retreat in a suburb of Chengdu, the noisy, sprawling capital of Sichuan Province. Luyeyuan roughly translates to "the open weald where deer run," and it references a venerated spot near Varanasi where the historical Buddha, having attained enlightenment, delivered his first sermon on the Dharma. This conception of the project as a temple in a clearing inspires much of the spatial narrative within and without.

With the natural boundary of the Fu River to the south, the trees and bamboo groves to the west of the 73,000-square-foot (6,770 m²) site segregate essential functions—car park, assembly areas, support buildings, lecture hall—as they create picturesque sequences of approach and egress. Access to the museum's primary entry on the west façade is through a narrow ramp, shaded by an arbor of existing trees and traversing a small pond as it gently ascends. Liu describes the experience of the central structure as a visit to an "underground palace," and the circulation plan accordingly emphasizes descent, the order of exhibits proceeding from the second to the first floor. The exhibition program spills out onto an open-air sculpture court that furnishes views of the water as it provides flexible event space.

In presenting an "inexorable, gigantic stone" solidly hewn out of concrete and shale brick, Liu forwards a dialogue between ancient statuary and modern architecture, casting both relic and reliquary as complimentary passages in the long history of man-made stone in China. Stretched over an elaborate structural system, the highly textured surface of the walls evoke carved or sculpted forms. The density of lateral impressions—articulated like the distinctive lamellar armor of the Tang Dynasty—is achieved by vertically pouring concrete against a formwork of brick common to the region, heightening the effect of a severe, even ascetic, realm. Glazed vertical slits exaggerate the play of light and shadow in the spaces within and afford only fragmentary glimpses of the bucolic surround without, as they segment the broad grey expanses of the north and south elevations into monolithic slabs.

Model view looking east

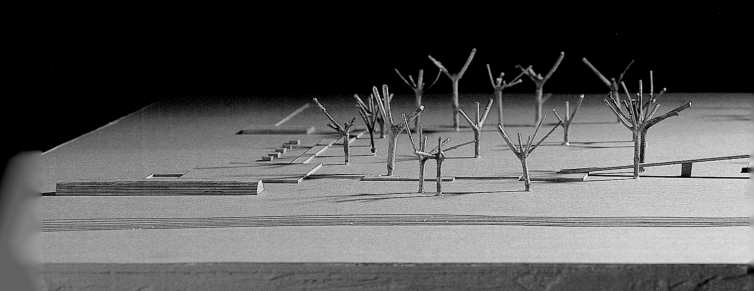

View of courtyard with display niches

Interior display cases

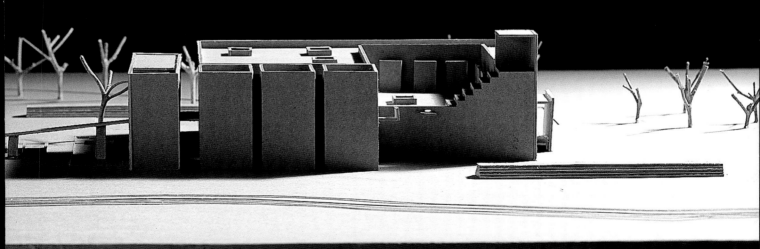

Model view of south elevation

XU TIANTIAN / DNA BEIJING

Inducted into the Asia Society's Asia 21 Young Leaders Forum in 2005, Xu Tiantian is founding principal of Design and Architecture Beijing (DnA Beijing), an interdisciplinary practice of city planning, urban design and architectural design. Xu received her Masters in Architecture and Urban Design from the Harvard Graduate School of Design in 2000, and her baccalaureate in architecture from Tsinghua University in Beijing. Prior to establishing DnA Beijing, she worked at a number of design firms in the United States and the Netherlands. She has also taught at the Central Academy of Fine Arts (CAFA) School of Architecture in Beijing. Her current research, Nomadic City, is a case study on contemporary migration and urbanization in western China.

DnA Beijing engages a broad scope of typologies, with commissions in both urban and rural environments. Projects currently under construction or in design development include the Inter Modal Transportation Point in Yantai City, Shandong Province (2006), the Ink Painting Museum in Inner Mongolia (2007), and the Songzhuang Art Center in Beijing (completed 2006).

DnA (Design and Architecture) Beijing / Xu Tiantian
Beijing, 2006

SONGZHUANG ART CENTER

The phenomenon of "painter's villages" in Beijing represents an important episode in the rise and rise of contemporary Chinese art. Now epitomized by the gargantuan, tourist-friendly Factory 798 at Dashanzi, these communities originally grew out of small, grassroots associations of painters, sculptors and performers—both schooled and self-taught—who were estranged from sanctioned venues for artistic expression. The first of these cooperatives were envisioned as entirely self-sustaining entities and obtained the necessary space for living, working, and presenting by adaptively reusing post-industrial structures and low-rent residential blocks at the periphery of built-up areas.

This tenacious pursuit of creative solidarity did not readily endear their authors to municipal bigwigs, however. Government organs such as the *China Youth Daily* described the more salient of these villages as, at best, "risky survival models" for aspiring young urbanites and, at worst, as sites for dissipation, mendicancy and anti-social habits of mind. But the ravenous domestic and international appetite for Chinese painting has, by and large, led to the wholesale mainstreaming of most of these countercultural guilds. The artists' proven ability to generate wealth for the towns and cities in which they have set up shop has had the ironic effect of not only reducing governmental meddling but in some instances, has led to direct state subsidy.

Songzhuang, some 50 miles (80 km) southeast of central Beijing in Tongzhou District, is easily one of the largest of these villages, currently supporting some 700 artists. There are several competing versions of the art colony's 1994 founding. The most popular version has a group of artists culpable for a number of "culturally sensitive" shows fleeing their former digs on the grounds of the ruined Old Summer Palace—in Beijing's western suburbs—for more permanent studio space. In time, the prodigious activity of this growing community attracted more and more artists, and by 2004, plans were in place to create a dedicated, public exhibition.

Set in the middle of a large plaza surrounded by low-rise sprawl, the functions of the new Songzhuang Art Center are confidently expressed in the building's exterior. The ground floor is contained within a peripteral colonnade of squat, white columns spanned by large panes of vision glass, revealing a flexible 27,000-square-foot (2,500 m²) space that can be utilized for a variety social events outside of the primary museum program. Punctuated by a number of courtyards, this story in turn supports an arrangement of four stepped, brick-clad volumes housing the exhibition spaces. Set back from the wide plinth defined by the lobby floor, the intersection between these two distinct zones provides the main horizontal axis as one approaches the building, and the physical heft of these massive red cubes belies the delicacy of the auditorium and galleries housed within. Lit by huge skylights, these triple floor-height rooms collectively supply some 12,000-square-feet (1,100 m²) of exhibition space and create an environment for art unlike any other in modern Beijing.

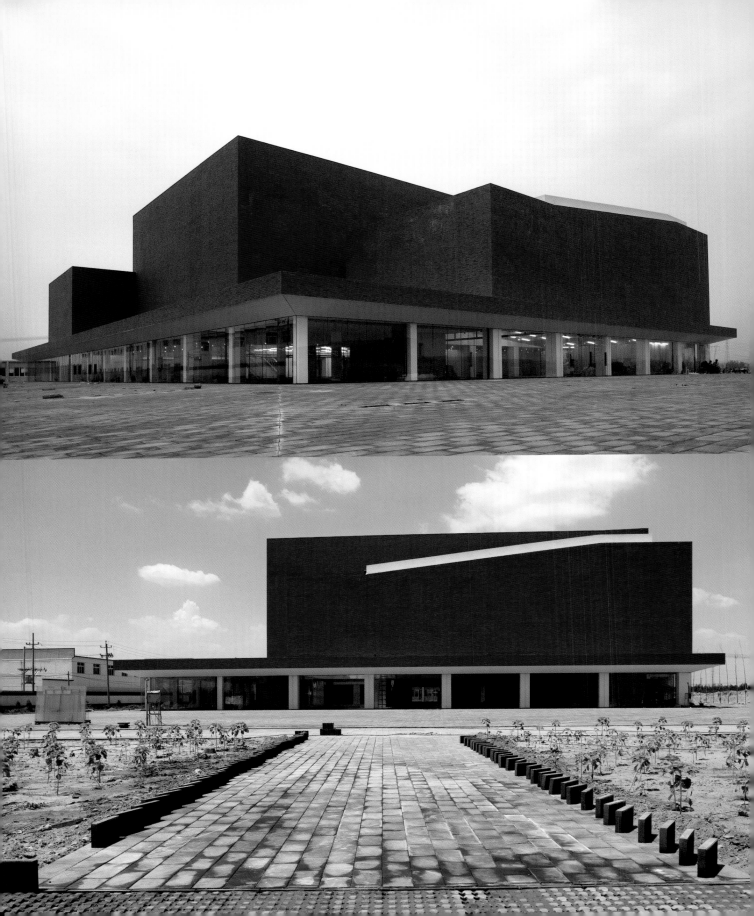

Section looking south

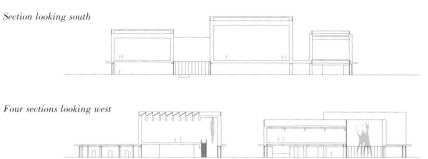

Four sections looking west

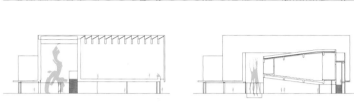

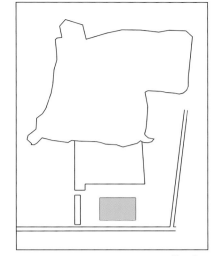

Site plan

Massing diagram: southwest view

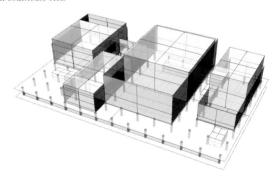

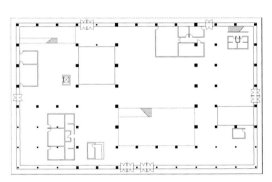

Second floor plan

Massing diagram: southeast view

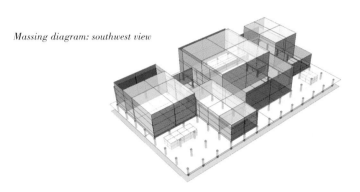

Ground floor plan

69

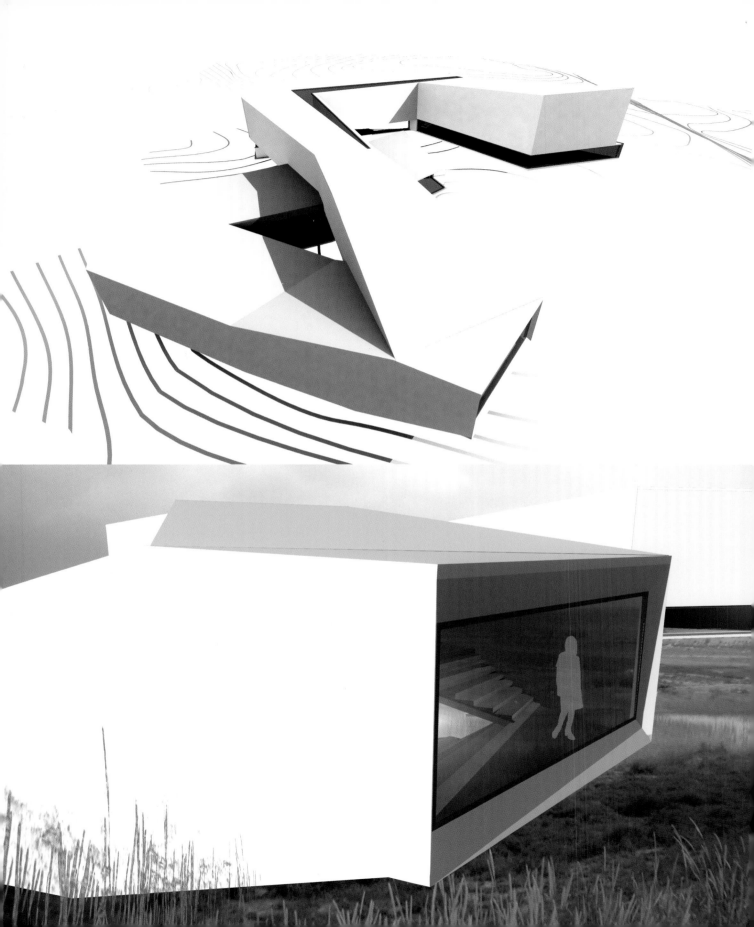

DnA (Design and Architecture) Beijing / Xu Tiantian
New Erdos City, Inner Mongolia Autonomous Region, Estimated Completion 2007

INK PAINTING GALLERY

A land of extreme climate and geography, the vast autonomous region of Inner Mongolia is home to some of the most remote urban concentrations on earth. Peopled almost exclusively by resettled Han Chinese, its twenty-five million souls inhabit a handful of dusty towns strung along the length of an administrative entity over three times the size of France. With ample natural resources, the region subsists chiefly on the extraction and processing of wool, coal, and geothermal power. In the last decade, an energetic public-private effort to visit the landlocked region with some of the bounty associated with the cities of the coast has lately called for a more diversified revenue base that sustains traditional industry as it encourages new sources of income. The new initiatives include the production of renewable energy—such as solar and wind power—and high-end manufacturing through the importation of the "High-Tech City" concept to the larger municipalities.

The national profile of corporations based in Inner Mongolia, such as Erdos Cashmere and Mengniu Milk—a dairy combine responsible for the Mainland Chinese variant of "American Idol"—have brought a measure of prosperity to the cities of the region, and Dongsheng, the seat of the prefectural agglomeration of Erdos, looks set for a major makeover. Hemmed in by the southern approaches of the Gobi Desert and by a U-shaped bend in the Yellow River, Dongsheng lies atop the Erdos plateau in the center of the province, its arid fastness mitigated by immense stretches of pastureland and a constellation of saline and freshwater lakes.

The ambition for Dongsheng to support an influx of high-skilled labor and an emerging middle class required a master plan that expands the old town into New Erdos City a few miles the south. Within a watershed dominated by gullies and small lakes, the new civic center is built around a lakefront museum as its chief city-making gesture. Funded by the private company managing the water resource, Xu Tiantian and DnA Beijing address the desolate beauty of the location with a serpentine ribbon of concrete straddling the uneven terrain.

Proposed as a showcase for ink scroll paintings and calligraphy, 22,600-square-feet (2,000 m²) of gallery and café program is distributed within an undulating form with a central span lifting clear off the ground, suggesting a desert viper winding over the dunes. Experientially, the space is conceived as one uninterrupted room, its stark white interiors interrupted only by the strategic application of two very large punched windows, offering cinematic views of the raw landscape. With the plan achieving a near-infinite loop, the height and width profiles vary along the length of the structure to suit a multiplicity of exhibition programs.

Elevations

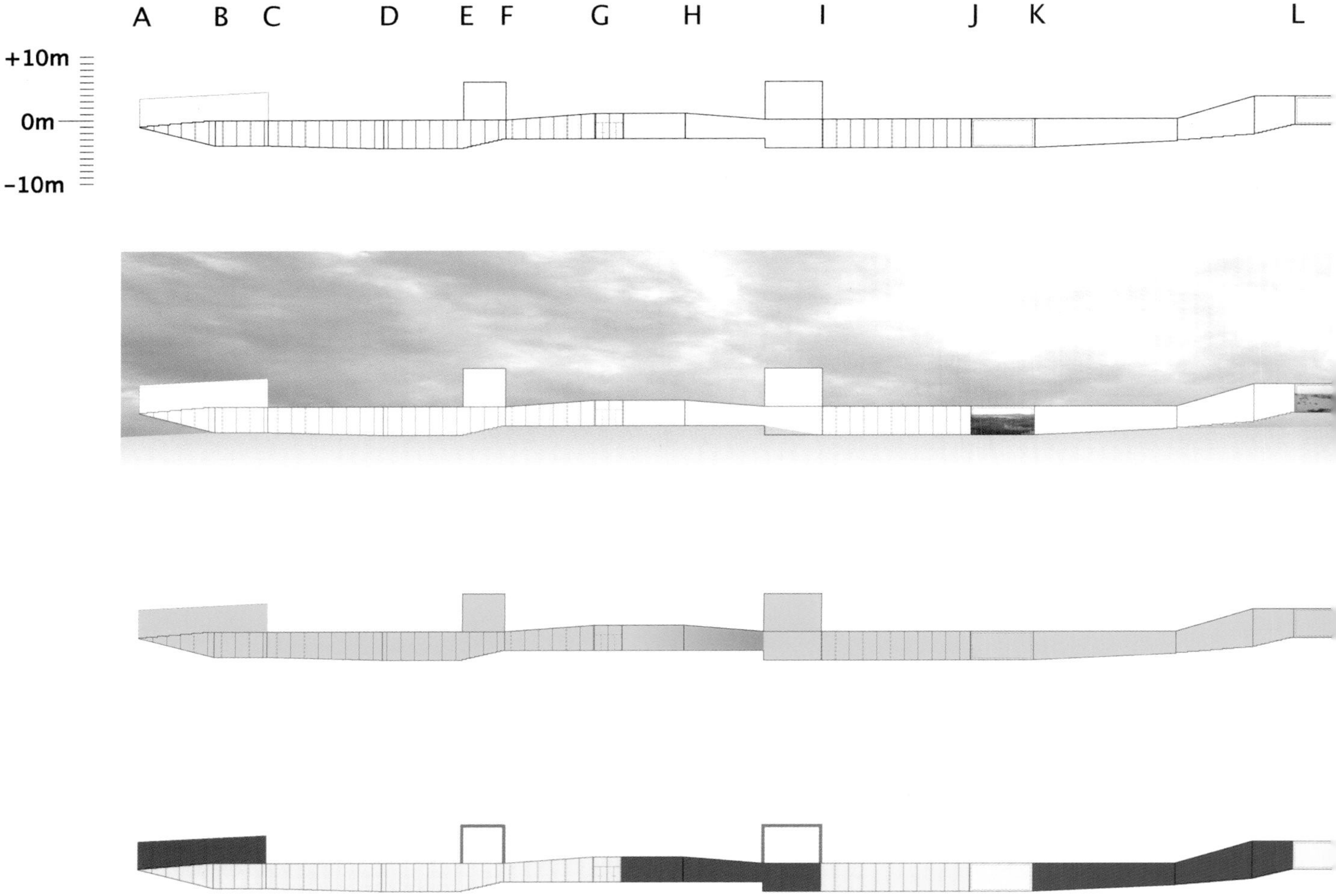

+10m
0m
−10m

A B C D E F G H I J K L

Site plan

Q P N O R M H G S I F E D C B A J K L

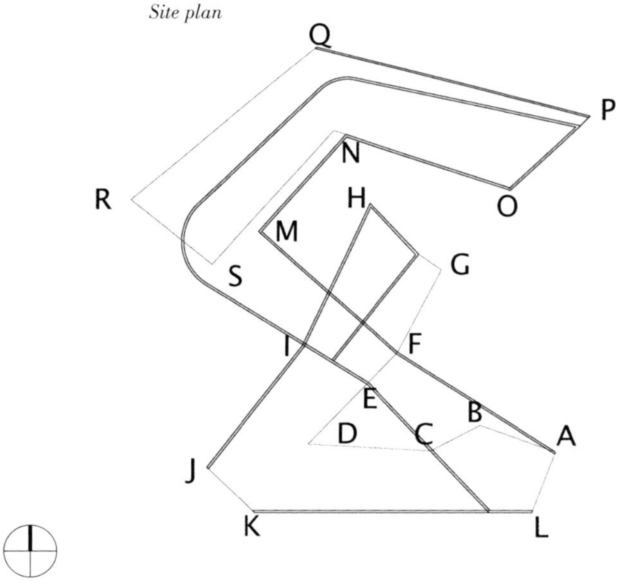

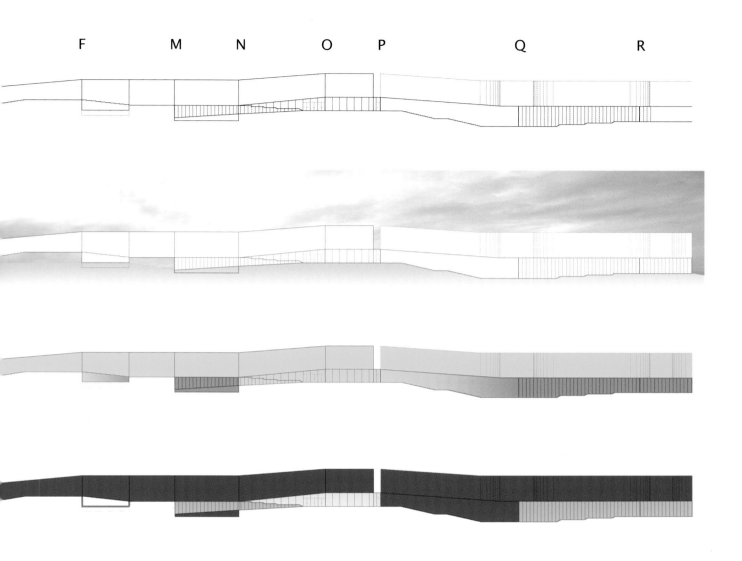

F M N O P Q R

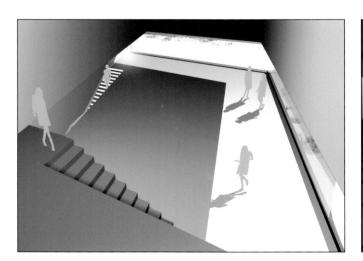
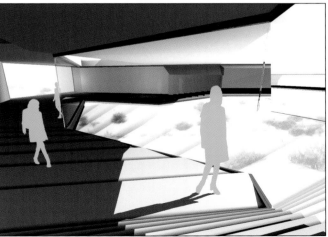

Interior views

YUNG HO CHANG /
ATELIER FEICHANG JIANZHU

Yung Ho Chang's return to China in the early 1990s after more than a decade in the United States is an event laden with many historic resonances. It is frequently characterized as a pivotal episode in the rebirth of modern architecture in China, due in no small measure to the simple fact that prior his founding of Atelier Feichang Jianzhu—with Lu Lijia in 1993—no private architectural studios had ever existed in the People's Republic.

With China undergoing unprecedented urban and suburban development—an intensive building process that is rapidly destroying the existing urban fabric and ecology, and threatening heritage and tradition—Yung Ho Chang holds that the true challenge for an architect working in the country today is to respond critically and positively to the current conditions of the boom: mega size, huge quantity, high speed, and chaos. The strategy of Atelier Feichang Jianzhu—literally, "unusual architecture"—is to focus on basic issues in order to resist losing architectural quality in the building craze. Atelier Feichang Jianzhu opposes mega with mini, re-emphasizing a humane and harmonious scale; quantity with the quality of both contemporary and traditional materials; speed with care, consideration, and critical thinking; and chaos with the ordered balance between urban development, ecological preservation, and a healthy respect for history and tradition. The studio's projects range from private houses to government institutions, from urban-scale proposals and exhibit installations to occasional experimentation with furniture and graphic design.

Chang was born in 1956, and studied at Nanjing Institute of Technology (now Southeast University), Ball State University, in Muncie, Indiana, where he received his masters in 1984, and the University of California at Berkeley, where he earned a bachelors degree in Environmental Design in 1983. He has taught at the architecture schools of Ball State, the University of Michigan at Ann Arbor, UC Berkeley, and Rice University in Houston. Chang has served as Dean and Professor of the Peking University Graduate Center of Architecture, held the Kenzo Tange Chair at the Harvard School of Design from 2002-2003, and, since 2005, as Professor and Head of Department at the school of Architecture at the Massachusetts Institute of Technology.

Atelier Feichang Jianzhu / Yung Ho Chang with Wang Hui
Beijing, 2003

PINGOD SALES CENTER / ART MUSEUM

The first decade of the 21st century finds Beijing's real estate free-for-all expanding well beyond the four teeming districts that traditionally made up its urban core, and should in short order fill out the zones created by the six (and soon, seven) vast orbital roadways radiating from the Forbidden City. Much of commercial development is dispersed along the middle rings, with the greatest concentration in what is now recognized as the Beijing Central Business District (CBD) to the east in Chaoyang District, between the 3rd and 4th ring roads.

Taking its name from a corruption of the Chinese for apple—*pingguo*—this major urban project by Yung Ho Chang anchors a residential community on the southern fringes of the CBD. Assigned the master plan for the 5.4 million-square-foot (500,000 m²) development by the Beijing-based Antaeus Group, the project brief also entailed the conversion of a former heating plant on the site into a sales office/showroom and contemporary art space with a total area of 30,000 square-feet (2,800 m²).

Allocated a modest budget and intended as a momentary structure, the scheme demanded a minimum of interventions to the weathered brick shell. But a number of key architectural insertions—including a series of expressively color-coded entrances and, most memorably, a flaring composition of unpainted steel grilles and no-slip ramps wedged into the north façade entrance—announce the new function of the building as they funnel visitors to a skylit, column-free, triple-height room carved out of the interior. These exaggerated shifts in scale and theme impart a mischievous character to the entire building. In transforming an industrial relic into a hybrid typology unknown to Chinese cities prior to "Opening and Reform," Atelier FCJZ gives meaningful form to popular aspirations suppressed by decades of austerity.

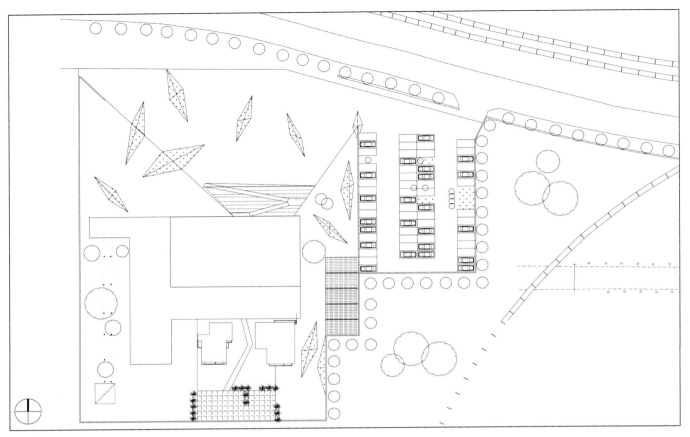

Site plan

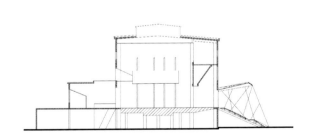

Section looking east

View looking south

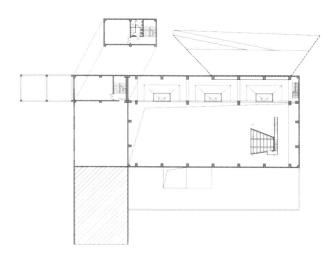

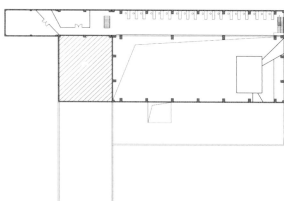

Third floor plan

Fourth floor plan

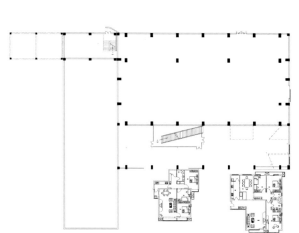

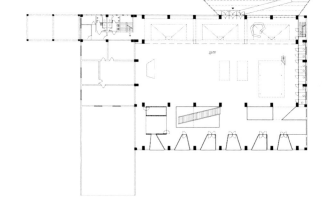

Ground floor plan

Second floor plan

Atelier Feichang Jianzhu / Yung Ho Chang
Beijing, 2002

SPLIT HOUSE

A clutch of villas on the floor of a wooded valley in Yanqing County, some forty miles (65 km) northwest of central Beijing, the Commune by the Great Wall remains the most recognizable of all the projects initiated by Zhang Xin and Pan Shiyi, the developer pair behind SOHO China. Envisioning the project as a showcase for contemporary Asian architecture, Zhang commissioned twelve design firms—mainly from the People's Republic, Japan, and Hong Kong—to create eleven private homes and a clubhouse in 2001. Seven years and 200,000 visitors on, the Commune is a fixture on the Beijing tourist trail, benefiting in no small measure from its proximity to the most popular stretch of the Great Wall at Badaling. Now operated by a German hotelier as a boutique franchise, with the smallest of the four- to six-bedroom homes renting at $1,500 a night in 2006, the development is the core of an even larger master plan that sees the addition of 21 more houses replicated from the prototypes.

The Split House is one of Yung Ho Chang's seminal constructions. A formal and tectonic critique of the *siheyuan*, or the traditional Beijing courtyard dwelling, its principal conceit of relocating an urban typology into a context of *shan shui*—mountain and water—is helped tremendously by the lush surround. 4,800 square-feet of program (450 m²) is distributed between two equal halves that diverge from a glazed entrance lobby pinned to the northwest of the hilly site. Creating a forty-degree angle that effectively separates the intimate functions of the house from the more public ones, the house draws the pristine landscape into itself, the existing copse of trees in the courtyard watered by a natural stream fortuitously discovered on the site.

The sustainable agenda extends well beyond scopic attributes, and provisions have been incorporated into design and construction to minimize its environmental footprint. Borrowed from a simple, millennia-old technique of fabricating houses from compacted soil and timber, the structure of the Split House is made of laminated wood and rammed-earth walls. In addition, the scheme is intended to be eminently flexible as the angle between the two wings is not fixed and can therefore be adapted to other sites in the valley. As the particular topographic conditions dictate the figuration of the plan, the Split House can morph into a Single House, Parallel House, Right Angle House, Bar House, or Back-to-Back House.

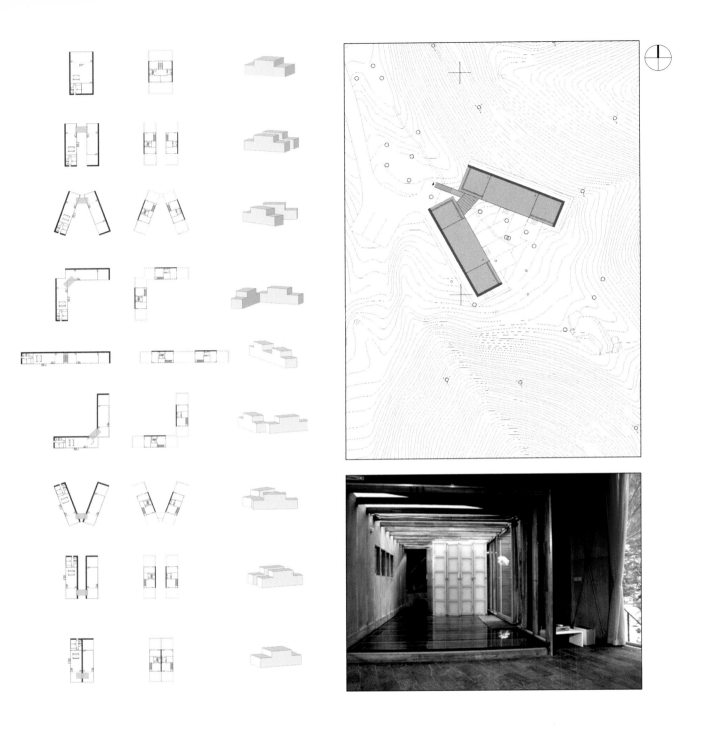

CLOCKWISE FROM LOWER LEFT: *Plan and morphology studies; site plan; interior view of connecting lobby.*

Second floor plan

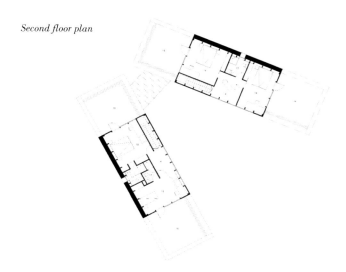

Ground floor plan

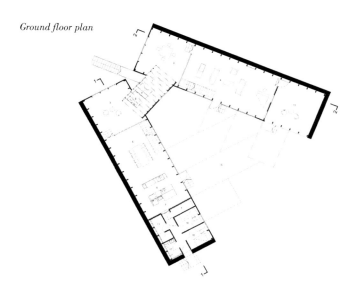

Sections looking west

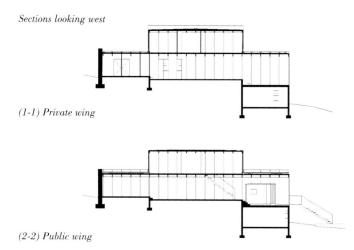

(1-1) Private wing

(2-2) Public wing

Atelier Feichang Jianzhu / Yung Ho Chang with Wang Hui
Beijing, 2004

VILLA SHIZILIN

In 2003, Yung Ho Chang was again tapped by a prominent developer couple who had recently charged his firm with an enormous residential master plan near the new Beijing CBD. The subsequent commission was only slightly humbler in spirit, and it demanded a suitable architectural focal point for the client's personal 52-acre (21 hectare) property in Changping District northwest of central Beijing, adjacent to the Ming Tombs and in the shadow of the mountains.

The brief sought an expansive 52,000-square-foot (4,800 m²) house for a small family, and required a diversity of programs—from a screening room and a recital hall, to a large indoor swimming pool—with the intention of reserving a number of these amenities as part of a private club. In devising a massing strategy, Chang exploits the majesty of the scenery by taking the telescoping views from an optical rangefinder as an organizing device, directing nine tapered spaces towards nine different views. The roofs slope to complete these "perspectival" rooms, interpreting traditional Chinese architectural forms into a rooftop topology. This creates a rolling artificial landscape that echoes the hilly terrain nearby. The structure of the building is a concrete sheer wall and beam system with local granite clad on the outside of the walls, indigenous brickwork, and dark cement tiles on the roofs.

The building site was originally a persimmon orchard, and a number of existing trees have been preserved in the sprawling plan of the villa, now encased in vitrine-like atria.

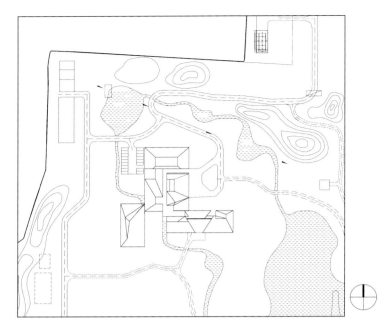

Site plan

East elevation

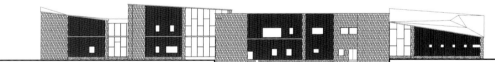

North elevation

West elevation

South elevation

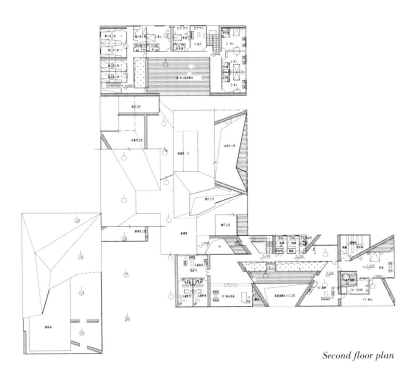

Second floor plan

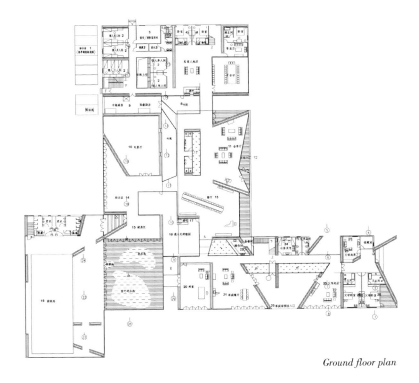

Ground floor plan

Atelier Feichang Jianzhu / Yung Ho Chang
Shijiazhuang, Hebei Province, 2004

HEBEI EDUCATION PUBLISHING HOUSE

Shijiazhuang, located two hundred miles (320 km) southeast of the twin megalopolises of Beijing and Tianjin, owes much of its modern existence to the steam engine. A rural settlement for most of recorded history, its development into one of the principal cities of the North China Plain only began with the intersection of two railway lines outside of town in the early 20th century. Situated at the junction of several north-south and east-west railroads by the time the Communist Party assumed unitary control over China, Shijiazhuang's status as a major transit hub contributed in no small part to its designation as the provincial capital of populous Hebei Province in 1968.

The present growth of local manufacturing industries has also brought the city a measure of prosperity, and the resulting demographic explosion saw its urban grid swell in all directions. One sure visual marker of the breadth of these changes is an incipient skyline. Chaotic and unremarkable, like those in a hundred other Chinese boomtowns, certainly, but the great and the good of Shijiazhuang have of late evidenced the spark of critical, citymaking ambition.

The owner and operator of this mixed-use tower by Yung Ho Chang is the local publishing combine. As the primary tenant, the Hebei Education Publishing House requires only three stories for its day-to-day running, but the lure of a bullish real estate market convinced the firm to build a twelve-story, 181,000-square-foot (16,800 m²) structure that combines a speculative office building with a multiplicity of cultural uses. With the editorial offices on the top floors, these programs boast a hotel, café, an indoor basketball court, art galleries—and of course, a full-service bookstore.

The formal concept of the building assumes a trabeated massing, with the principal volumes composed of a low-rise plinth supporting two broad posts, surmounted by a three-story lintel shuttered in wood. The void between the two main vertical volumes is portrayed as a "vertical garden" accessible to the public, and it contains essential services such as fire stairs. The depiction of this interstitial space as the connective fabric between several discrete "communities" supports the conception of the project as a "miniature city."

Seventh floor plan

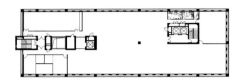

Twelfth floor plan

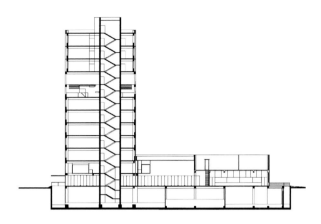

Section looking west

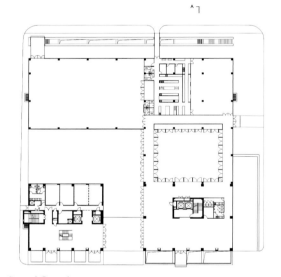

Ground floor plan

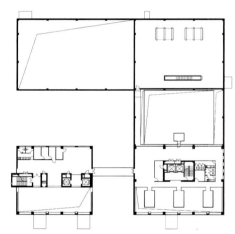

Second floor plan

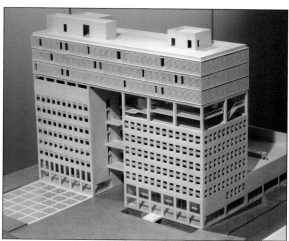

CLOCKWISE FROM TOP: *South elevation; model viewing southeast; model viewing northeast.*

ROCCO YIM / ROCCO DESIGN

Assuming a vital, mediatory role between East and West, Hong Kong architects have long provided an intravenous means of technology transfer for the People's Republic since the earliest years of "Opening and Reform." That the founding of Rocco Design and its predecessor firm coincided with the establishment of the first Special Economic Zones in 1979 proved to be an auspicious coincidence. Under the direction of Rocco S. K. Yim, the last thirty years saw Rocco Design become one of the most prolific practices in the former Crown Colony, and the first decade of the 21st century sees the firm's Mainland China portfolio aggressively making up for lost time.

The geographic spread of Rocco Design's projects in China have moved well beyond the readily accessible region around Hong Kong and the Pearl River Delta, to include a number of riverine housing master plans, with one in Hainan Island for the Beijing developer SOHO China (Boao Village, 2001) and another in a western suburb of Shanghai (Jiu Jian Tang, 2005). But his most important commissions to date remain close to home, in Guangdong Province. Yim's 2004 commission for the massive prefectural museum in Guangzhou was secured after an invited international competition that included entries from Peter Eisenman, Coop Himmelb(l)au, UN Studio, Hans Hollein, and Eric Owen Moss.

Rocco Design / Rocco Yim
Shanghai, 2005

JIU JIAN TANG VILLA

This 8,000-square-foot (750 m²) villa is part of 46-unit, low-density residential development planned for a site on the east bank of the Huangpu, deep in Pudong District. Based on the spatial organization of a traditional courtyard dwelling but realized on a slightly grander scale, this reimagined *siheyuan* draws on a rational tendency already present in vernacular Chinese architecture. Rocco Yim steers clear of slavish revivalism, however, allowing the evolving demands of 21st-century living to inform the design. The result is a residence that is comprehensively modern, and one that can be easily adapted to a number of possible configurations.

A low whitewashed wall provides a hermetic enclosure to the entire composition, shielding the residents from the din of the street, as it provides a framework for the spaces within. The plan integrates a processional sequence through two main courtyards, divided by high volumes containing the principal program spaces and linked by ambulatories and side rooms to the west and east. Entered through a breach in the north wall, the forecourt is a stone causeway flanked by square ponds to the left and right, formally announcing visitors to the communal areas of the villa. This paved walkway—also the site's central axis—continues uninterrupted through the main block. The living and dining rooms effectively occupy a two-story glass house-within-a-house, shielded to the north by an angled, interlocking grille of aluminum tubes—that by turns suggests a tile or bamboo roof—and shaded on the south-facing side by a screen of wood slats. A second water-court leads to a second volume, that while identical to the first in form, diverges in function as it comprises the private quarters.

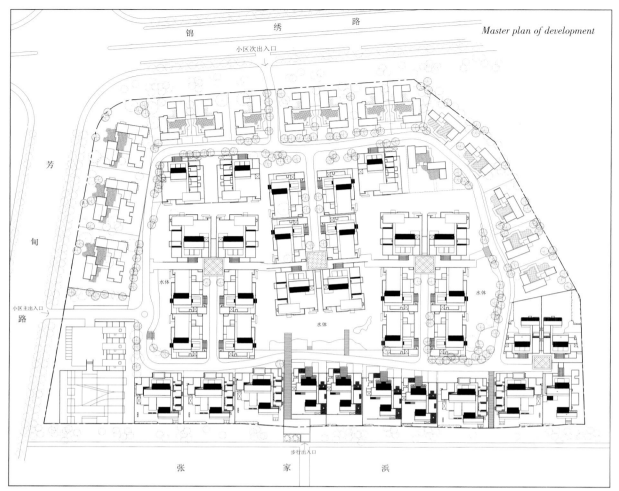

锦　绣　路

Master plan of development

小区次出入口

芳

甸

路

小区主出入口

水体

水体

水体

步行出入口

张　家　浜

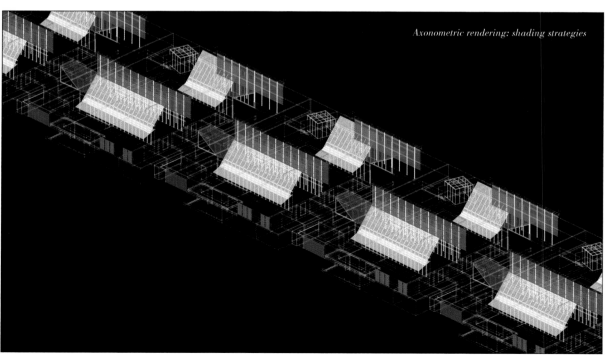

Axonometric rendering: shading strategies

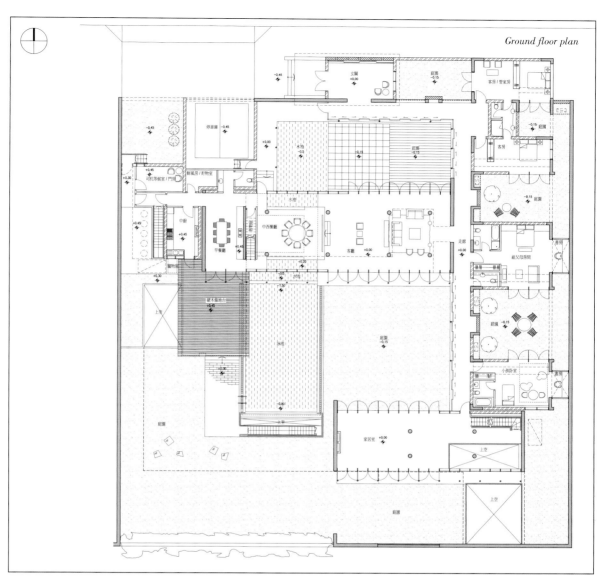

Ground floor plan

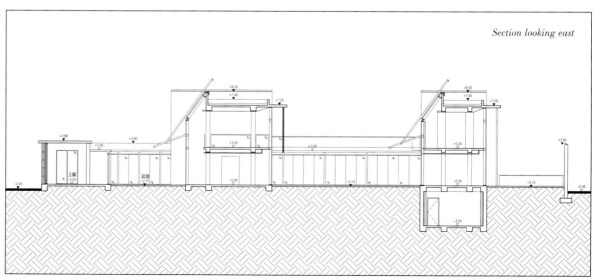

Section looking east

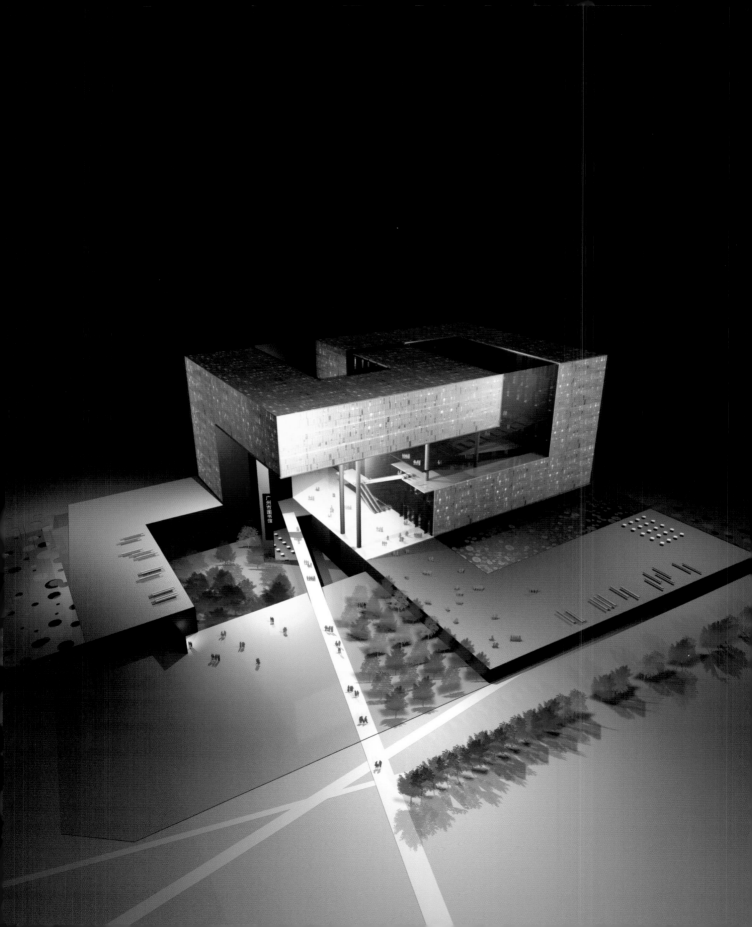

Rocco Design / Rocco Yim
Guangzhou, Guangdong Province, Design Completed 2005

LIBRARY OF GUANGZHOU

The capital of the richest province in the People's Republic, Guangzhou remains the most historic of all the cities on the Pearl River Delta, and has arguably spent the last half-century coasting on its reputation as the Canton of yore. Increased economic competition from parvenu municipalities like Shenzhen and Zhuhai—abutting the Special Administrative Regions of Hong Kong and Macau respectively—has, however, forced Guangzhou to reassert its preeminent role as a political and cultural center of the region.

Through the agency of the all-powerful Guangzhou Urban Planning Bureau, the city initiated a massive urban renewal scheme at the turn of the century. Much of this effort is concentrated on the building of a new city center—Zhujiang New Town—that by 2010 will boast one of the more extravagant assemblages of civic buildings in all of China. Set on a grid defined by wide boulevards, the bevy of planned structures include Guangdong Science Center, the Guangzhou No. 2 Children's Palace school complex, Zaha Hadid's 1,800-seat theater for Cantonese opera, and the Guangdong Museum by Rocco Yim, all of which are slated for completion by the end of the decade.

This competition entry—also by Rocco Design—was proposed for a site to the east of the Culture and Art Square, an open space along the main north-south axis of Zhujiang New Town. The Library of Guangzhou is intended to replace a Sino-Soviet edifice in the old city, and Yim imagines the new structure as an intricate puzzle. The massing concept is expressed in two interlocking forms looming over an expansive sequence of low platforms and the street below. Reaching a height of over ten stories, the architects cast the meta-dialogue between several seemingly oppositional shapes as an attempt to balance the "relationship between extroverted and introverted spaces."

The iconic building achieves an elaborate plan as it rises, subtly recalling the calligraphic layers of a multi-stroke ideogram. The variable circulation patterns on each floor correspond to specific functions within the project brief, creating detached spaces for special collections, and open plans for circulating libraries, public spaces, and other amenities. Public access to the building, through a long ramp on the southeast corner, provides a dramatic means of ascent into the heart of the building, with elevated plazas and escalators negotiating the voids between volumes.

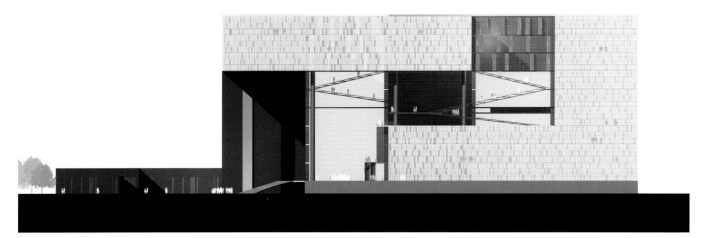

South elevation

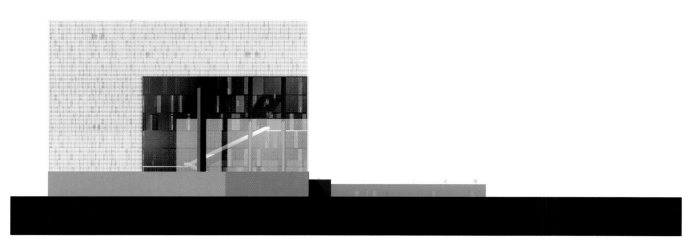

West elevation

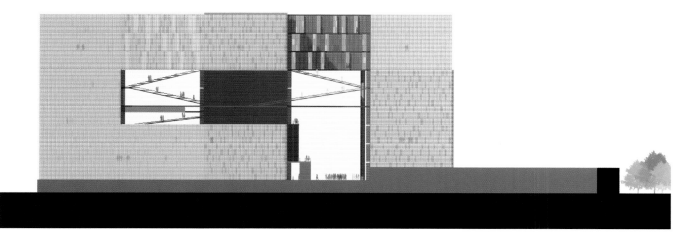

North elevation

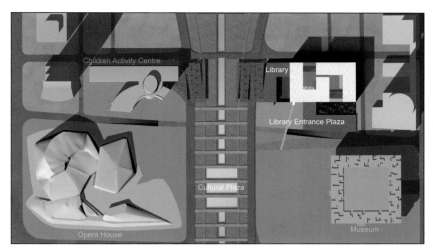

Site plan

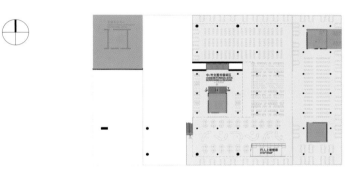

Third floor plan

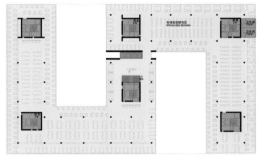

Ninth floor plan

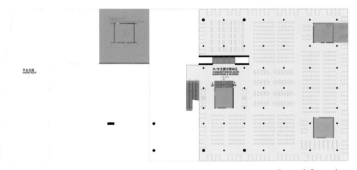

Second floor plan

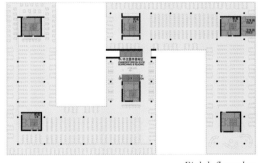

Eighth floor plan

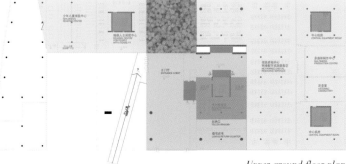

Upper ground floor plan

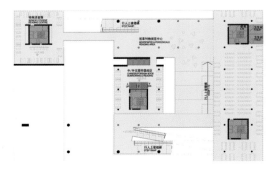

Fifth floor plan

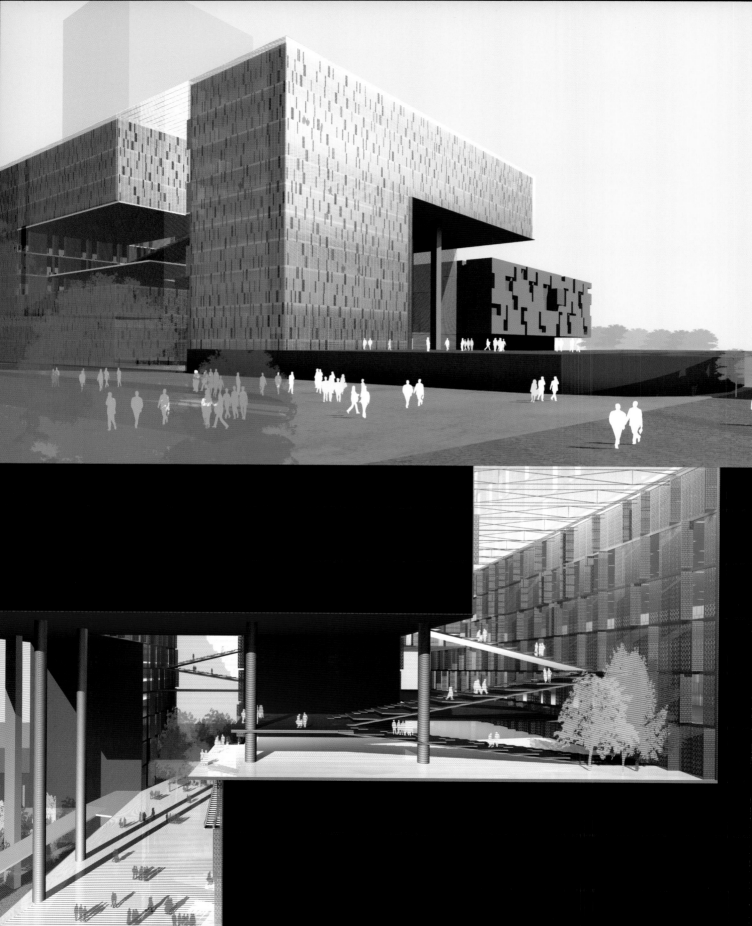

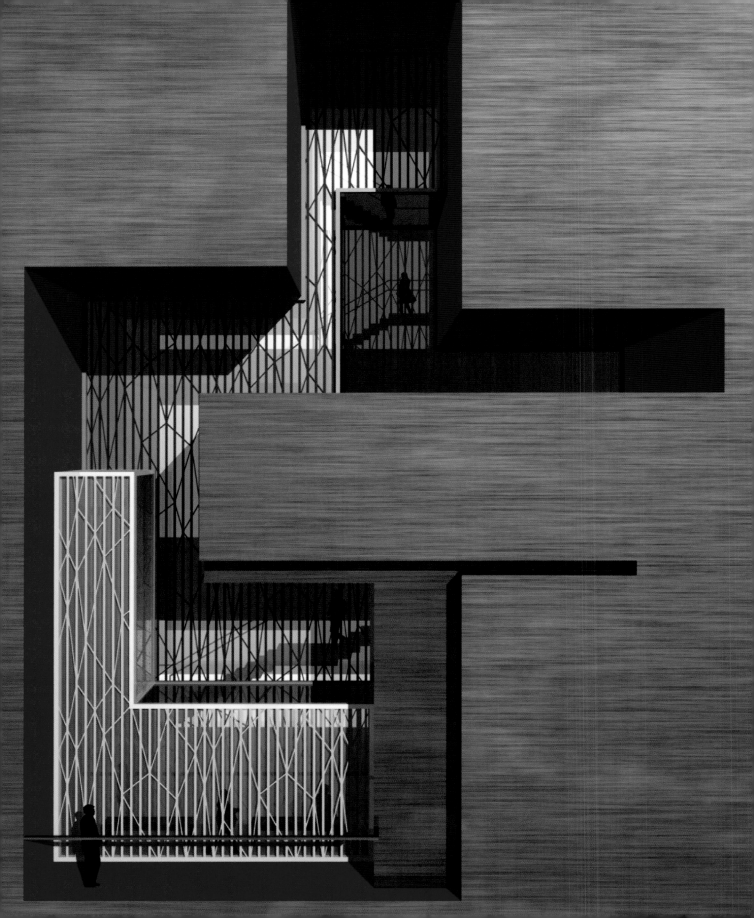

Rocco Design / Rocco Yim
Guangzhou, Guangdong Province, Estimated Completion 2007

GUANGDONG MUSEUM

This companion project to Zaha Hadid's Guangzhou Opera House up the street provides an altogether distinct contemplation of form and function, an orthogonal straight man to Hadid's spectral prankster. Awarded to Rocco Design in 2004, the formal and spatial strategy of the Guangdong Museum draws direct inspiration from the ornately carved boxes of wood, lacquer, or jade used in East Asia for millennia as repositories of precious items. A variation on this genre of functional art objects is the nested Chinese box, which not unlike the Russian *matryoshka* doll, provides a perfect metaphor for graduated layers of enclosure. As the provincial museum for Guangdong, this 646,000-square-foot (60,000 m²) museum incorporates a number of thematically distinct exhibition programs—in effect, four institutions in one. With the variety of items proposed for exhibition ranging from reconstructed fossils of large Cretaceous-era dinosaurs to installations of contemporary Chinese art, the spaces are organized in modules that could be freely adapted to accommodate differing requirements.

The plan is arranged around a six-story atrium in the center of the building. Points of access to the four main halls—natural history, Chinese history, art, and temporary exhibits—radiate from this great room, with connections to a dedicated research facility, office, retail, café, and service functions. Appointed with a maximum provision for natural light, high ceilings, and the open circulation paths demanded by modern galleries, the porous qualities of the interior contrast with the material density of peripheral core and the exterior skin. Expressed on the highly articulated surfaces of the cube, alcoves and views out to the city are periodically inserted in the circulation plan to ease potential "museum fatigue."

Section looking east

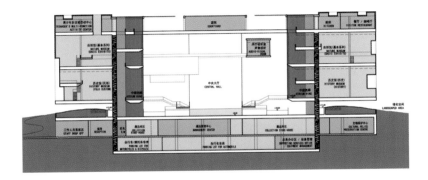

Upper ground floor plan

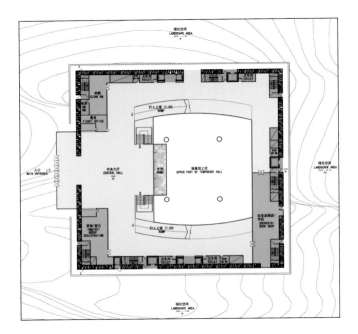

West elevation

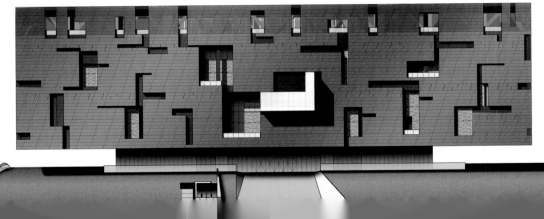

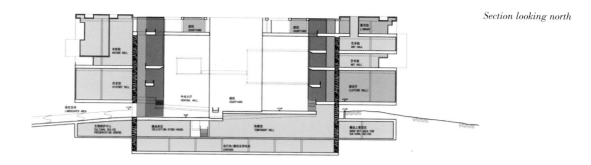

Section looking north

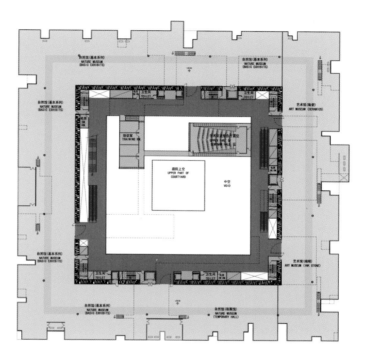

Third floor plan

North elevation

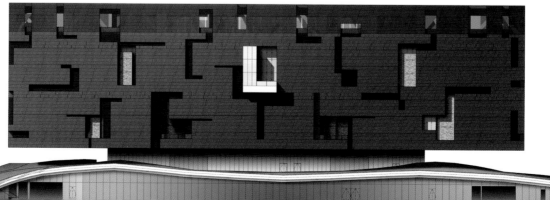

AI WEIWEI / FAKE DESIGN

A prince among China's reigning *enfants terribles*, and a spiritual godfather to the next generation, Ai Weiwei's career as architectural provocateur continues to expand the formal and programmatic vocabulary he first established with the design of his own brick house in the suburbs of Beijing in the late 1990s. Situated just off the 5th ring road, one of the most telling aspects of this split-level cube built out of crude grey brick is the absence of a wall to conceal the bathroom. Declaring that such a spatial device was merely decorative and therefore unnecessary, he allegedly quipped that the room's relegation to the second floor was "privacy enough."

With a recent portfolio that is by turns mischievous, darkly comic and thought-provoking, Ai endows the planning and execution of spaces with the same restless, unstinting spirit that drives much of his work as a conceptual artist. His spare design approach also draws heavily from the sensibilities of editor, social critic and satirist, fashioning a series of environments that require the presence, comprehension and the thorough participation of its end users. One of the more poignant of these signature works, from 2001, is a granite memorial park in Zhejiang Province to his late father, the poet Ai Qing—whose humiliating "reeducation" in labor camps during the Anti-Rightist purge and the subsequent Cultural Revolution indubitably played a part in the young Weiwei's unsentimental education.

Born in 1957 in Beijing, Ai studied at Beijing Film Academy. During a long sojourn in New York City, from 1981-1993, he attended the Art Student's League, and the Parsons School of Design. Thereafter, he was also active as an editor of avant-garde journals, including a series of "internal documents" on Chinese modern art and contemporary culture: the *Black Cover Book*, the *White Cover Book*, and the *Grey Cover Book* (1994, 1995 and 1997, respectively). Ai's subsequent architectural work—including the much-ballyhooed "birds nest" for the 2008 Olympics to which he was famously retained as artistic consultant to Herzog & De Meuron—is conceived and realized through the vehicle of FAKE Design.

FAKE Design / Ai Weiwei
Jinhua, Zhejiang Province, 2001

YIWU RIVERBANK PARK

Some two hundred miles southwest of Shanghai, Jinhua is a riverine city on the make. At some remove from the coast and ensconced in what the municipal website describes as "a land flowing with milk and honey," the local economy is rather staked on the manufacture of pharmaceuticals and construction materials, and the long-term ambition of its city fathers is to raise the city's commercial profile well beyond its lazy provincial bailiwick. The centerpiece is an improvement of the waterfront along the Yiwu, a tributary of the Qiantang River, and is part of a raft of capital projects. These presently include an architectural park featuring seventeen follies by a number of prominent Chinese and Western design firms, with a master plan also undertaken by FAKE Design.

Ai Weiwei's earliest project for the municipality, Yiwu Riverbank Park, is intended as an intermediary between old Jinhua and the new city gathering mass across the river. With the park straddling both sides of the Yiwu, Ai devised a serrated embankment in plan and profile, dominated by a repeating sequence of stepped, triangular forms. Hacked from the tough, indigenous granite and quilted now and then by patches of lawn grass, these stand sentinel over a network of paved stone paths and the water beyond.

The forest of freestanding stone piers on the southern bank that appear to break out of the regimented gardens of stone proclaim that the park is also a belated memorial to Ai Qing, one of Jinhua's favorite sons—and the designer's late father. Ai Qing was the principal *nom de plume* of Jiang Zhenghan, one of the most important Chinese poets of the modern period. Denounced as a Rightist in 1958, and exiled with his young family to a series of punitive farms in the wastes of Xinjiang province, he was freed only after thirty years of humiliation and hard toil. He passed away in 1996.

The park's easy appeal to pedestrians and weekend strollers notwithstanding, the formal idiom harnessed here is clearly born of quiet severity and contemplation. Indeed, the warm hues acquired by the stone during the day, and the combination of both pyramids and obelisks denote a Nilotic tomb, its angular, unadorned forms sturdily built and directed ever upward. Born out of a son's duty to his father, the implicit, even spiritual, desire for redress transcends the unrelentingly material universe of Chinese socialism, and hints at the critical motivations that impel much of Ai Weiwei's art and architecture. He has expressed as much: "The Chinese people have gone through a lot and if it is merely about more cars and tall buildings, then it is not worth it."

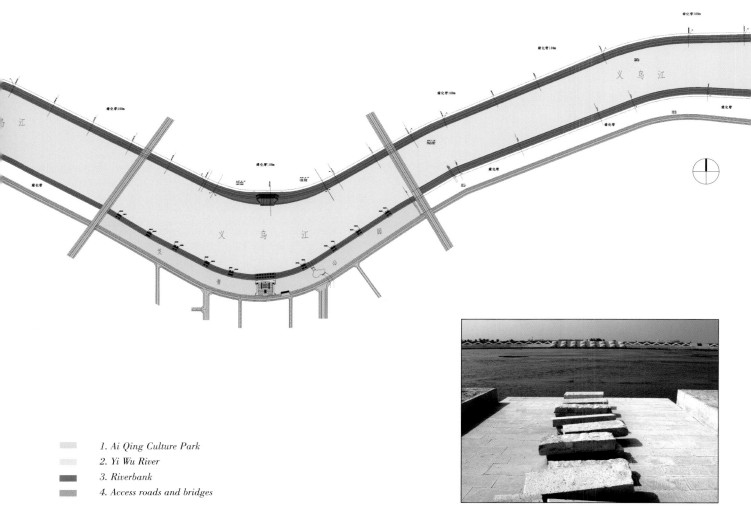

义乌江

义乌江

义乌江

艾　青　公　园

1. *Ai Qing Culture Park*
2. *Yi Wu River*
3. *Riverbank*
4. *Access roads and bridges*

Construction view with cut granite slabs

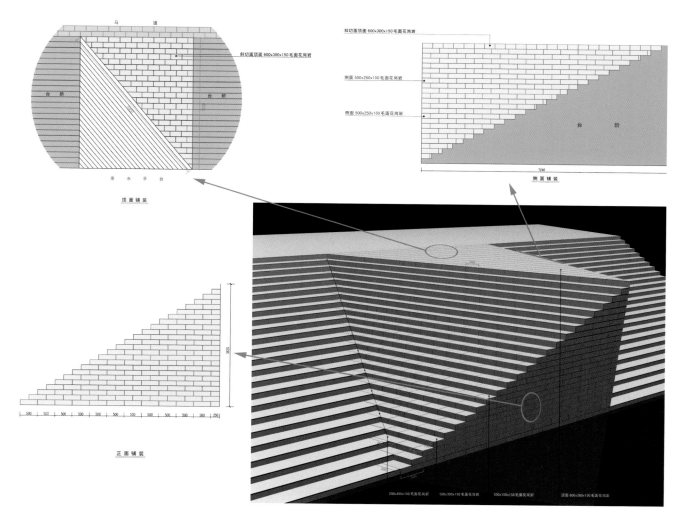

斜切面顶面 600x300x150 毛面花岗岩

斜切面顶面 600x300x150 毛面花岗岩

马　道

台　阶

台　阶

亲　水　平　台

顶 面 铺 装

侧面 500x250x150 毛面花岗岩

侧面 500x250x150 毛面花岗岩

台　　阶

7240

侧 面 铺 装

500　500　500　500　500　500　500　500　500　500　250

正 面 铺 装

900x450x150 毛面花岗岩　　500x300x150 毛面花岗岩　　500x150x150 毛面花岗岩　　顶面 600x300x150 毛面花岗岩

Stone coursing diagrams

147

FAKE Design / Ai Weiwei
Beijing, 2004

NINE BOXES

With the design of this project, Ai Weiwei crafts a viciously clever response to the pandemic of gated communities blighting the periphery of the capital. The client acquired a huddle of small, one- and two-story residences—realized mainly through the lethal application of Sino-Postmodernist gestures in clay tile, bluestone, and concrete stucco—and proposed converting them into nearly 30,000-square-feet (2,751 m²) of art gallery and office space. Armed with a limited budget and even less time, Ai Weiwei set about his appointed task with characteristic aplomb, and exorcised the vaguely Mediterranean ghosts on the site by immuring them in sheaths of galvanized steel sheet tacked onto simple structural frames. Organized around a pond, the nine boxes themselves become ciphers, refracting and diffusing the colors of the surrounding landscape with the changing seasons.

Site plan

Existing conditions

Box A-N: Ground floor plan

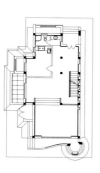

Box E-N: Ground floor plan

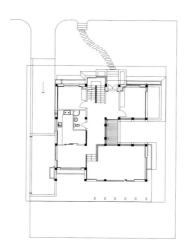

Box G-N: Ground floor plan

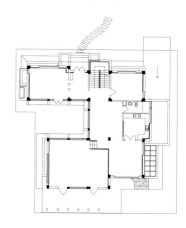

Box A-N: South elevation

Box E-N: South elevation

Box G-N: South elevation

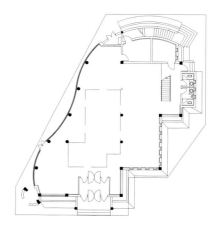

Box F-S: Ground floor plan

Clubhouse: Ground floor plan

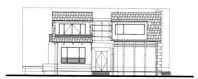

Box F-S: South elevation

Clubhouse: South elevation

FAKE Design / Ai Weiwei
Beijing, 2004

WHERE TO GO RESTAURANT

FAKE Design deploys a playful application of commonplace building materials to create a one-of-a-kind Beijing hangout. Situated near the foreign legations along the eastern 3rd ring road and just south of the National Agricultural Exhibition Center in Chaoyang District, this 2,480-square-feet (230 m²) restaurant was built in forty days and rehabilitates an existing structure on the site.

The key interior and exterior effects are generated through the use of laminated cement fiberboard. Each a foot (300 mm) wide and half-inch (10 mm) thick, thousands of these panels are sandwiched together and suspended on a metal frame to form the walls. Materializing like tears on the surface of the south façade, shards of clear glass inset into the composite wall—and compacted together in the same way as the cement boards—permit only obscured views of the dining areas and minimize the amount of natural light in the space. The overall experience of an unfinished room is further enhanced by the use of furniture constructed out of medium-density fiberboard and the willful exposure of service functions. A revolving program of contemporary paintings acts as a foil.

Ground floor plan

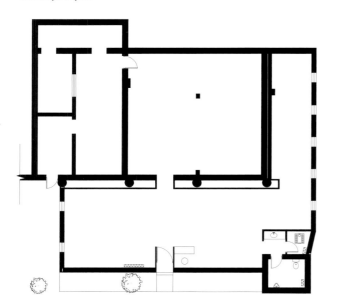

GARY CHANG /
EDGE DESIGN INSTITUTE

Although manifestly urban, Gary Chang's portfolio is not one of soaring office towers for big corporate clients, but instead focuses attention on the quality of space. Chang accounts for the multi-dimensionality of an urban setting: his designs are fluid and variable—common outdoor accoutrements move inside to become interior landscapes.

While much of Hong Kong's—and increasingly, the cities of Mainland China's—architecture is dominated by large firms and governed by developer and statutory constraints, Chang is more interested in crafting architectural narratives. Born in Hong Kong in 1962 and receiving his degree in architecture from the University of Hong Kong in 1987, Chang founded his own company, EDGE Design Institute HK, Ltd., in 1994 after apprenticing with a local firm. In addition to his major cultural and educational commissions, Chang's firm has applied his innovative philosophy to domestic design; among other small-scale projects, EDGE created the Kung Fu Tea & Coffee Set for Alessi.

In 2000, Chang held his first solo exhibition at the Hong Kong Arts Centre. That same year, he was among the first group of representatives from Hong Kong to be invited to participate in the International Architecture Exhibition in Venice, and the invitation was again extended in 2002. Since 1995, Chang has held a teaching post at the University of Hong Kong.

Edge Design Institute / Gary Chang
Shenzhen, Guangdong Province, 2004

CRC CITY CROSSING PROJECT SHOWROOM

This off-site sales office for one of the largest commercial development schemes in metropolitan Shenzhen belies a more urbane functional brief than the one concealed by its pedestrian name. Leases to the biggest Western-style mall in the city are certainly issued within its lavish, candy-colored enclosures, but its expandable program owes much to the diverse typological interests of the client. Inserted into the lower levels of a boutique hotel operated by the same patron, this split-level showroom leads a double life.

Devoted to hawking tony real estate during the day, and with a full complement of marketing and support programs—including a seminar room for press conferences—the space effortlessly converts into a full-service lounge and bar at night. This built-in flexibility also suggests that this temporary showroom can become a more permanent fixture as an extension of the hotel once space in the shopping complex is fully let.

In plan, the area allotted for the showroom is divided between a 970-square-foot (90 m²) first floor and a 2,900-square-foot (270 m²) second level. Gary Chang transforms the space into a double-height atrium. The focus of this hollowed out room is unquestionably a grand staircase—encased in an armor of colored glass and acrylic plates—that spirals visitors up to a rectangular hall carved out of the remainder of the upper floor. Adorned with a wall of scale models, the adaptability of this hall is enhanced by the introduction of modular furniture, also designed by Edge. Fundamentally a swivel chair appointed with either a light box or a built-in computer console, these fluorescent orange cubes divide the floor area into a compact grid, but roll out to different seating configurations when necessary.

Edge Design Institute / Gary Chang
Guangzhou, Guandong Province, 2003

APARTMENT AT CANNES GARDEN

The emergence of an urban middle class in China has eased the enforcement of the infamous one-child policy to a significant degree, but its effects still cast a long shadow over the planning of domestic spaces. This 1,900-square-foot (110 m²) intervention is essentially an existing three-bedroom unit in a typical high-rise residential development, but the client brief for this project demanded the conversion of the extra bedroom into a study for a couple. Unshackling this spare room from its designated purpose, Edge Design and Gary Chang explored its latent potential, and used the liberated space as a central point from which to redefine the relationships between all the rooms in the apartment. In the design of this project, Chang "was particularly interested in leaving clues to trigger more interaction and to allow different combination of spaces in the light of giving more freedom in domestic living," creating a condition of perpetual imminence "in which normal and unexpected activities could unfold."

The agent of surprise here is a huge wall cabinet hung on a pivoting hinge, which when at rest, seals the envelope of the study as it addresses the living and dining areas. When this movable wall is deployed, the erstwhile bedroom can be open on three sides, leaving half the apartment barrier-free. Once all the operable panels are set back to their closed position, the unit reverts back to a conventional three-bedroom.

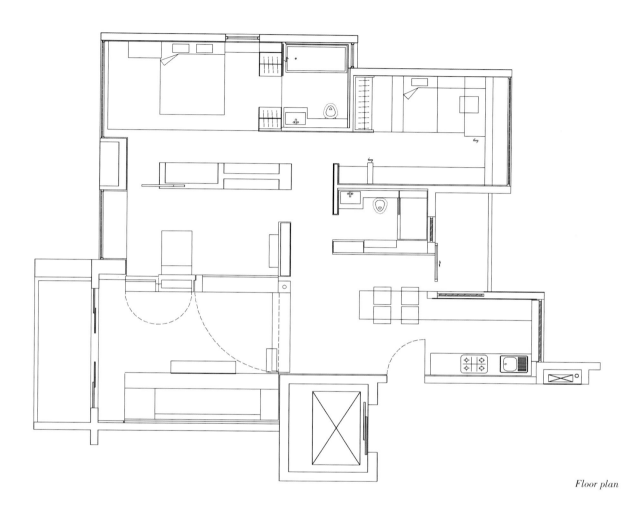

Floor plan

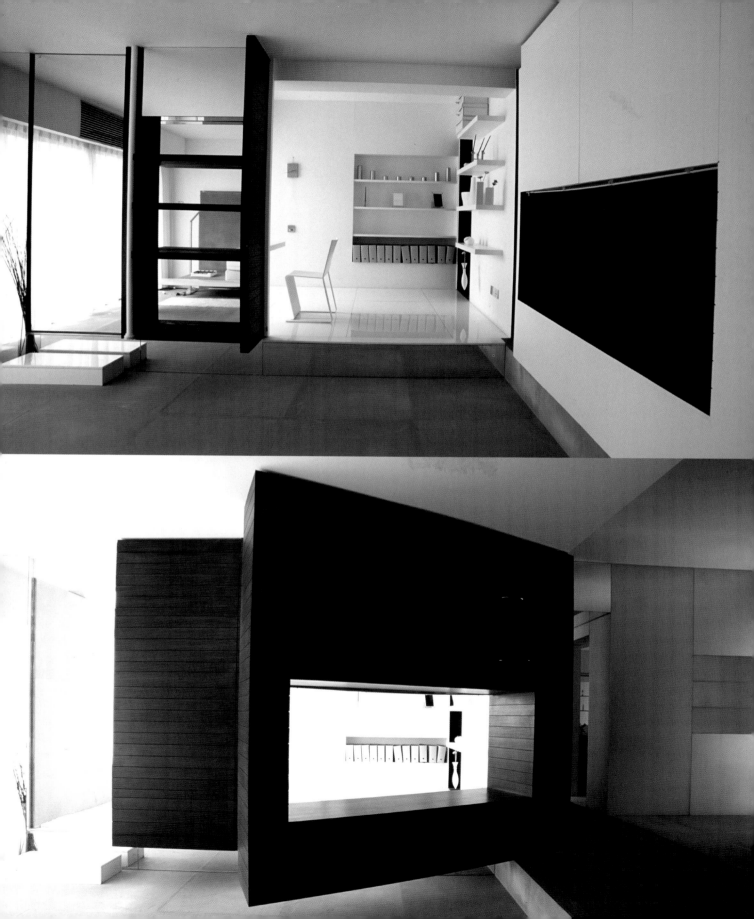

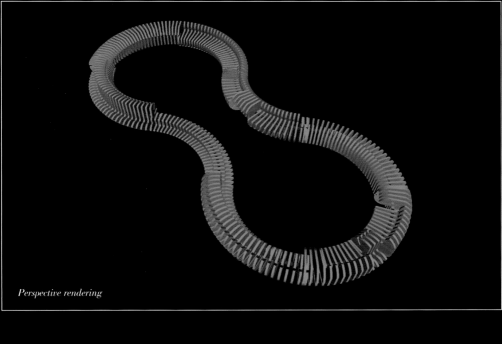

Perspective rendering

Edge Design Institute / Gary Chang
Hong Kong SAR / Variable Locations, 2004

LEISURE SLICE

Designed for a plaza within the Hong Kong Arts Centre (HKAC) on the Wanchai waterfront—but ostensibly adaptable to any open public space—this project is an attempt at recreating a common public amenity. Fusing an art object with street furniture, Leisure slice was conceived to be interactive rather than merely visual. A segmented construction made up of timber slices connected to steel anchors, its constituent parts could be rotated and deployed to create new functions. Accommodating various modes of seating, ad-hoc tabletops, and even a "bed" that museumgoers could lie down in, the project physically extends the activities of the HKAC beyond the assigned programs contained within its physical plant.

MA QINGYUN / MADA S.P.A.M.

MADA s.p.a.m—fully *Ma Designers and Architects: strategy, planning, architecture and media*—is the Shanghai practice founded by Ma Qingyun in 1999. Headquartered in a former state-run primary school and with an official website emblazoned with big red stars, the firm is not all ashamed to exploit high socialist camp in branding its identity. The product of Ma's admittedly "transcultural, cross-pacific" and media-savvy background, MADA's stated mission is to be an active and critical voice in the new architecture, confident in its "capability to resolve real building problems and fulfill social/political aspirations."

MADA's professional remit engages a broad spectrum of disciplines, from urban planning to interior design, with a broad client base in both the public and private sectors. And the studio is nothing if not prolific, with a current portfolio that boasts a dozen projects either nearing completion or well underway, in typologies ranging from cultural institutions, single-family residences, to speculative commercial and residential developments. Recent constructions include the Zhejiang University Library in Ningbo, Zhejiang Province (2003); Qingpu Thumb Island, in Shanghai (2006); Father's House (2003); and Courtyard House (2005), both in Xi'an, Shaanxi Province.

Born in Xi'an in 1965, Ma Qingyun received his bachelors degree in architecture from Beijing's Tsinghua University in 1988 and his masters in architecture from the University of Pennsylvania in 1991. Prior to his return to full-time practice in China, Ma worked in the American firms of Kohn Pedersen Fox and Kling Lindquist in the 1990s, and established a predecessor to MADA in 1995, with the MRMADA Agency in New York City.

MADA s.p.a.m. / Ma Qingyun
Shanghai, 2004

EDGE GARDEN

Located in Qingpu District, this project is a series of modern interventions intended to preserve a historic Daoist site dating from the 18th century from encroaching development. Adjacent to a temple to the protector deity Chenghuang—literally, "the town god"—only the traditional gardens within the precinct survive intact, the shrine having been stripped of most of its confessional significance and relegated to an extension of the municipal museum for most of the Communist era. Enclosed within a white wall with distinctive tile eaves, Qushui Gardens—literally meaning zigzagging channel—typifies an aesthetic in indigenous landscaping that replicates in miniature natural features like mountains and lakes.

Edge Garden was conceived by Ma Qingyun as a sequence of prefatory and processional spaces that lead into a south-facing portion of the Qushui Gardens. Formally, Ma describes the project footprint as "four parallel bands: a pedestrian boulevard, the waterside promenade, the flood control canal, and the [edge] park" inserted on the Qushiu side. Transitional devices are used to connect the four main elements, with the provision that the new additions be welcoming to the public and remain distinct from the historic precinct but impose as little as possible on the existing structures.

In a material and figurative sense, the flood control canal, with all the ritual cleansing properties associated with water, segregates the gardens from the larger commercial area. The canal is negotiated through two simple footbridges, and contact with the water itself through a tactical arrangement of three stairways on the north bank. Informed by principles of Chinese geomancy, the designers position each stair "in such a way as to complement the design and flow of the surrounding environment." Two of the stairways are placed facing each other along the promenade closest to the canal, and the combination of these effects generates for visitors the illusion of treading over water.

The waterway is then an active participant in the experience of the new park and its Qing Dynasty antecedent. Projecting from the embankment at a right angle, the third stairway and its allied forms mimic the concrete-and-steel canopy suspended over it, which the designers set up to anchor to the entire composition on the eastern fringes of the site. As it makes contact with the water, this stair terminates a sweep initiated by the crown of the canopy, formally linking the contemporary pavilion to the canal. A concrete guardian taking after the spiritual one lost to history, this low canopy—unambiguously modern in form and hue—sustains the forward movement of the ancient covered walkway as it undulates horizontally.

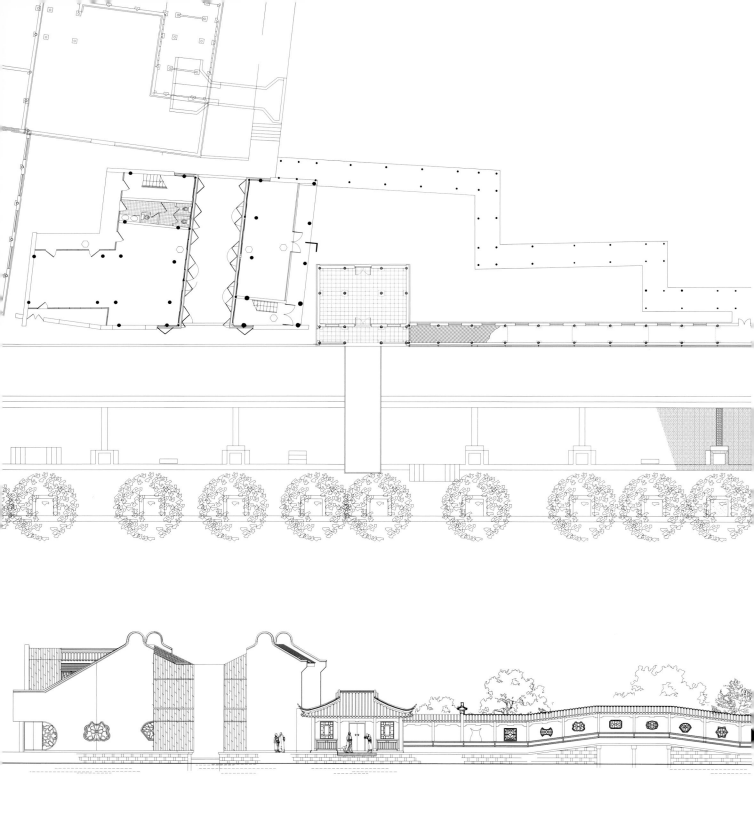

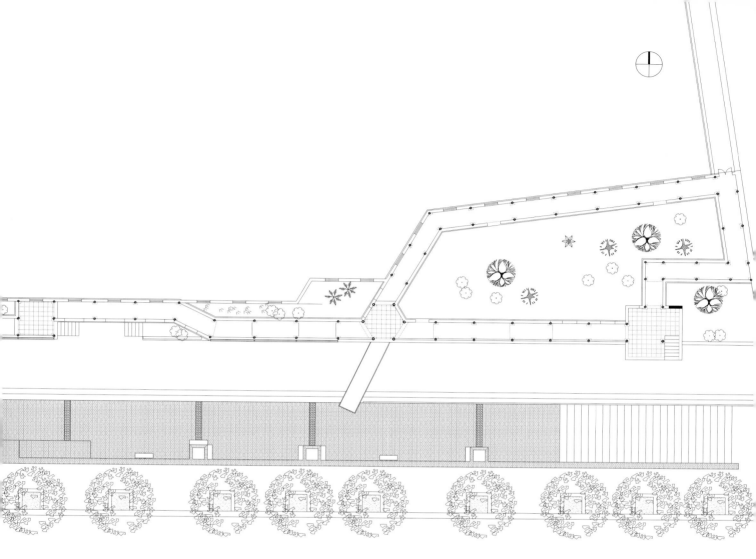

Site plan

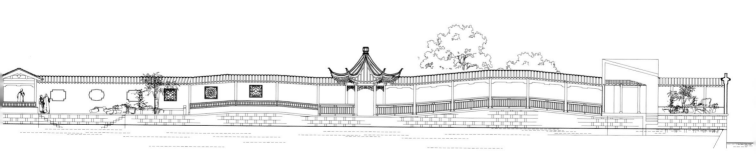

South elevation

MADA s.p.a.m. / Ma Qingyun
Shanghai, 2005

RED STAR KINDERGARTEN

In the late 1960s Red Star became the name of the most popular primary school system in Shanghai, roughly equivalent in ubiquity to the big-box chain stores of the present day. With the recent emergence of competitive private pre-schools, the Red Star system comprehensively fell out of favor, and most of its school buildings were abandoned. MADA s.p.a.m. is not only obsessed with high socialist nostalgia, but also fascinated by the opportunity to engage the urban dislocation caused by the wholesale obsolescence of many state-run enterprises and institutions.

Ma Qingyun engaged in the complicated effort of turning this 8,600-square-foot (800 m²) kindergarten into an architectural studio. The original building has no particular design but evinces a unique type of socialist modern hybrid, injected with a mawkish attitude toward the design of spaces for children. The architect kept in check the banal but appositive qualities of the building's formal and functional idiom by wrapping it with a new skin. This sheath is then constantly violated to either suggest new functions or reveal the original white tiles. MADA employs a signature material for the exterior cladding system—compressed bamboo board, which is frequently used in China as a framework for concrete but in this instance is individually framed in stainless steel. The desire here was to create something that was neither a corporate practice nor an atelier. It is rather a combination of production house and exhibition space, with wide apertures for natural light and a fluid circulation plan. The building was conceived with a number of memorable means of vertical ascent; one of its interior features is a very wide stair that also doubles as an impromptu auditorium

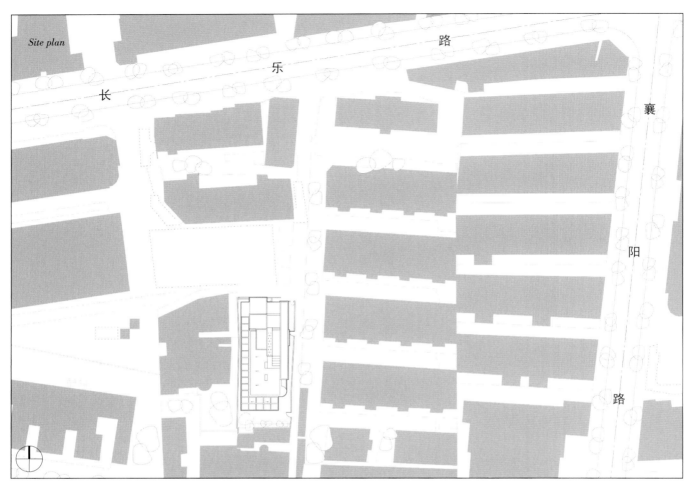

Site plan

长 乐 路

襄 阳 路

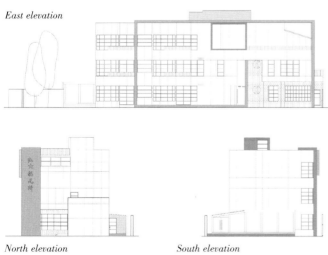

East elevation

North elevation

South elevation

View of main staircase from the third floor

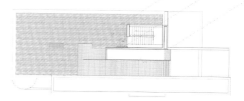

Roof plan

Third floor plan

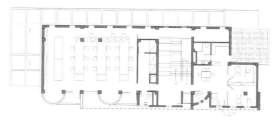

Second floor plan

Ground floor plan

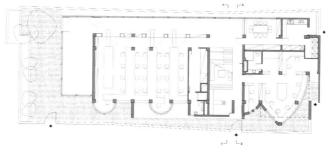

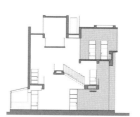

Section looking south

Section looking north

MADA s.p.a.m / Ma Qingyun
Shanghai, Design Completed 2004

GEM ON THE BUND

The Bund, the principal waterfront of Shanghai's west bank, is now utterly entombed in the shadow of Pudong's stratospheric skyline. But what the Bund lacks in height, it more than makes up for in character. Studded with architectural relics from a bygone era when the city was a concession to the Western powers, the rehabilitation of the early steel-frame buildings along the embankment have again restored the street's prewar luster. Once the commercial heart of Puxi—the old city—the Bund now appears to be the exclusive domain of boutique hotels, high-end shops, and restaurants.

This mid-block, six-story, 73,000-square-foot (6,770 m²) project flaunts a slightly less commercial but all the same flamboyant program. Planned as a temporary structure, Gem on the Bund is the multidimensional billboard for the 2010 Shanghai World Expo, a civic fête that is second in propagandistic importance only to the 2008 Beijing Olympiad. Proposed as the information, education, and media center for the fair, its relatively compact form is entrusted with a Shanghai-sized brief: to display "the world's achievements in science and economy and China's achievements in civilization and culture." As in the World's Fairs of the past, this will be communicated using state-of-the-art technology. The work of specially commissioned media artists—projected on practically all the vertical and horizontal surfaces of the structure—presents potential visitors, and passersby on Zhongshan Road, with dynamic, ever-changing vistas.

The structure is basically a hybrid of rigid, structural cores and a load-bearing glass façade. Individual glass segments are linked together to form a robust structural system. The key concept that drives the structural design is redundancy. Mounted on a lightweight but sturdy frame, the building is designed to remain standing even with up to two-thirds of its panels removed.

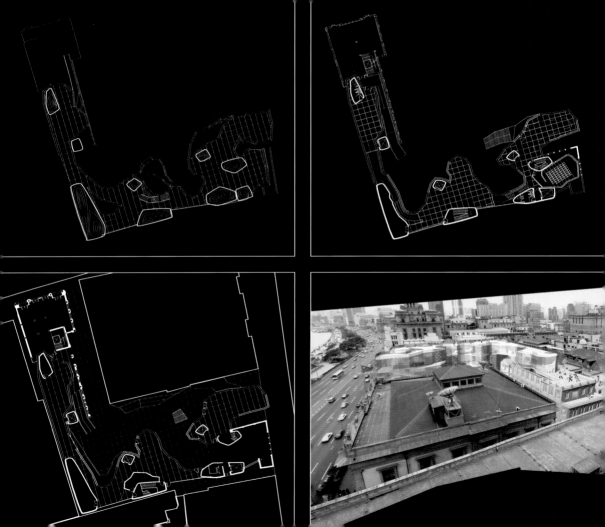

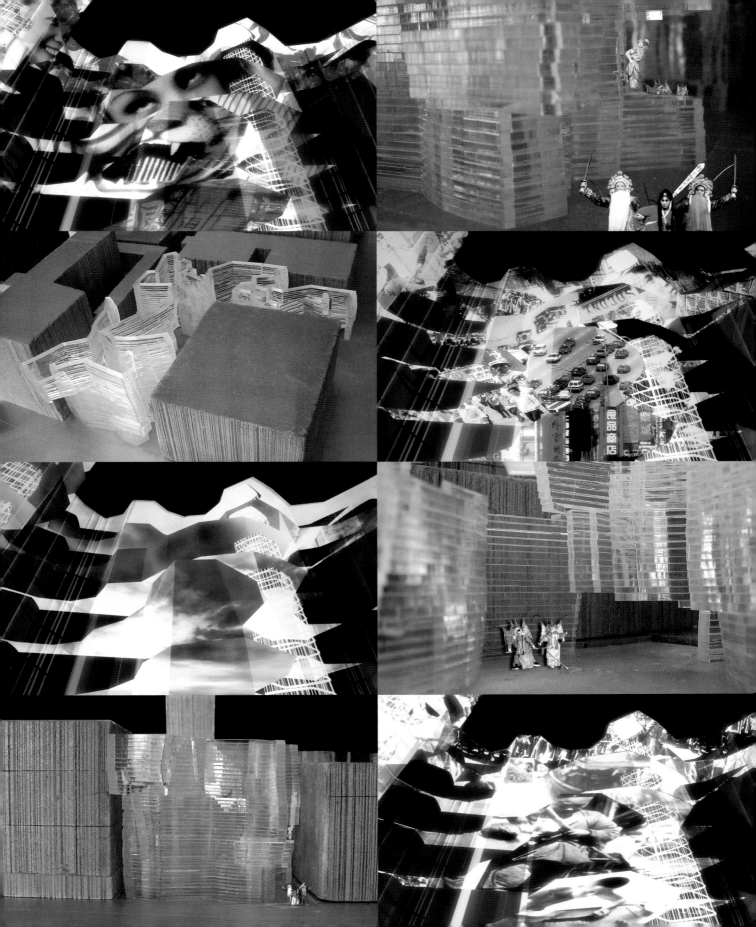

ZHANG LEI / ATELIER ZHANG LEI

The former imperial capital of Nanjing lies at the intersection of several geographic and economic axes. Roughly between Guangzhou and Beijing, it is often also seen as the psychic divide between the underdeveloped interior of the country and hyperdeveloped Shanghai to the east. With greater Nanjing growing at a relatively measured pace, Zhang Lei—a native son of Jiangsu Province—feels right at home in this mid-level boomtown. Noting that an architect's philosophical disposition and consequent work habits "are inevitably more or less integrated with the city he lives in," Zhang esteems the opportunity "to work calmly and modestly."

With a portfolio of projects focused mainly on the cities of the Yangtze and Pearl river drainage basins, the principle at the heart of Atelier Zhang Lei's mission is the resolution of problems with the most reasonable and direct methods of construction. The firm responds to requirements of adaptability with an inventive use of locally available materials appropriate for the humid climate of the Southeast China region. Coupled with a deliberate environmental agenda that strives to conserve natural resources already imperiled by accelerated industrialization, each of the firm's proposals introduce visual templates with shared compositional attributes and details, emphasizing elegant, simple forms, ample ventilation and ease of circulation.

Zhang Lei was born in 1964. He completed his baccalaureate and masters in architecture from the Nanjing Institute of Technology (now Southeast University) in 1985 and 1988, respectively, and continued his postgraduate studies at ETH Zurich through 1993. He has taught at Southeast University, ETH, and the Chinese University of Hong Kong. Since 2000, he has served as Professor of Architectural Design at Nanjing University and principal of Atelier Zhang Lei.

Completed and current projects by Atelier Zhang Lei include dormitories for the Dongguan Institute of Technology in Dongguan City, Guangdong Province (2004); The Qiandai International Mansions Showroom in Shanghai (2006); and a proposed house for CIPEA (China International Practical Exhibition of Architecture), in Nanjing (2006).

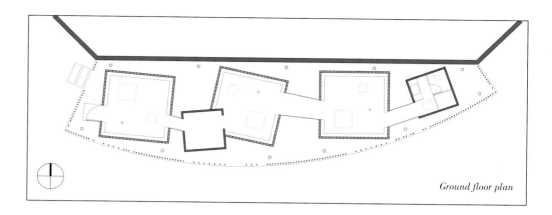

Ground floor plan

Atelier Zhang Lei / Zhang Lei
Shanghai, 2006

QIANDAI SHOWROOM

This pavilion, a combination of concrete, bamboo, and glass block, addresses the intersection of two streets in Qingpu, a suburban district to the southwest of the skyscraper forests of Shanghai proper. Set up as a showroom for adjoining residential tower blocks—the Qiandai International Mansions—the tiny 1,600-square-foot (150 m²) structure provides an elegant solution to a straight-forward functional brief.

Consisting of five small rooms, the material palette Zhang Lei employs directly corresponds to the program—with three rooms clad entirely in glass block containing the sales offices, a wooden box serving as the restroom, and with the final stone box encasing the scale model of the development. Braced in unfinished concrete, these three main materials also constitute the curtain wall of the Qiandai towers. Bamboo stakes, wrapped tightly around the curving edge of the street to screen the exterior, are a tectonic subversion, as the material often only appears in the vernacular urban context as mere scaffolding.

Atelier Zhang Lei / Zhang Lei
Nanjing, Jiangsu Province, 2003

OFFICE AND LAB BUILDING
MODEL ANIMAL RESEARCH CENTER

The capital of China for no less than six imperial dynasties and one short-lived republic, Nanjing is psychically hobbled by the passage of its historical moment, relegated for some time now to second-city status in the East China region by the relentless Shanghai juggernaut. But the city's storied reputation as one of China's great intellectual centers remained impervious to this decline in political prestige, and the jewel of its higher-education system, Nanjing University, is quite possibly the oldest continually existing institution of its kind in the world. Founded by the Wu emperor Sun Xiu in 258 AD as the Imperial Central College—*Nanjing Taixiue*—its present incarnation is well attuned to the demands of an emerging local and national economy.

Situated in one of the state-mandated High-Tech zones erected around the city, this research facility is operated by Nanjing University's Pukou campus and funded by the Ministry of Education. Dedicated to the advanced study of genetics, circulation through the 83,000-square-foot (7,770 m²) office and laboratory building was generated in part by the collaborative nature of the work conducted by the professors and their student assistants. Zhang Lei, who had previously completed a multilevel dormitory complex for the university, employs an open layout unusual for Chinese academic structures and draws a number of planning and gestural devices from progressive residential and office design.

In plan, the U-shaped building is conceived as an interlocking sequence of public spaces both within and without. Housed in a double-height corridor along the main north-south axis, six staircases link the various functions from a porous central spine. This narrow hall and other transitional areas within the program—illuminated by generous skylights and punched windows in a variety of configurations—establish an inviting, light-suffused environment for researchers to interact. The exterior courtyards, patterned after traditional Chinese gardens, correspond with the open plan of the interiors.

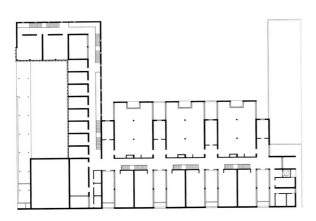

Second floor plan

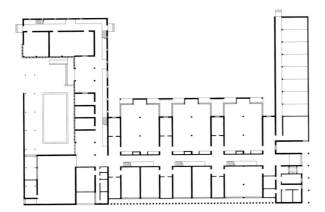

Ground floor plan

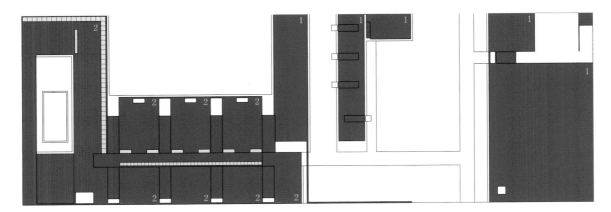

Site plan

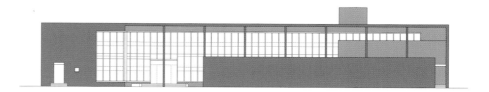

South elevation

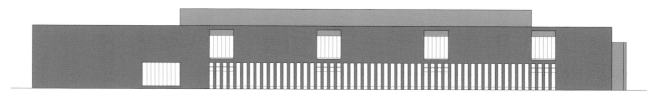

East elevation

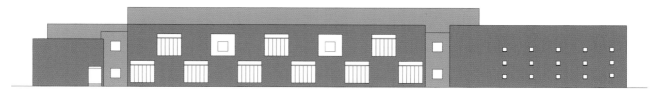

West elevation

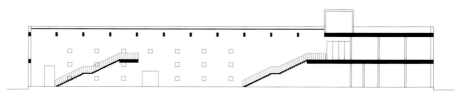

Section looking north

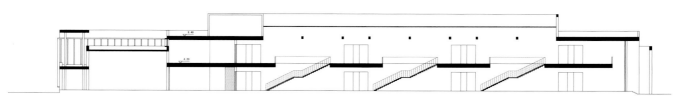

Section looking west

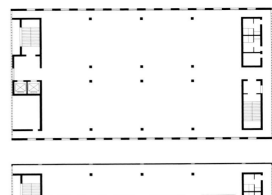
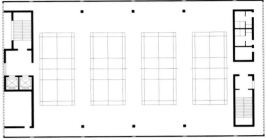

CLOCKWISE FROM LEFT: *Site plan; typical floor plan, badminton courts plan.*

Atelier Zhang Lei / Zhang Lei
Nanjing, Jiangsu Province, 2005

JIANYE SPORT MANSION

Set within the dense Nannhu neighborhood just south of central Nanjing and east of a bend in the Yangtze, this nine-story project overlooks a recreational park dedicated to area residents. The brick-clad building, faced on its sides with aluminum, incorporates nearly 108,000-square-feet (10,000 m²) of mixed program. Shops are set up on the ground floor, offices on the second floor and there are seven stories of athletic facilities.

The variety of openings on the exterior accommodates the diverse uses within. The floor heights themselves correspond to specific functional requirements. The top floor, for example, is thirty feet (9 meters) high for badminton, while the eighth floor for table tennis achieves a twenty-foot (6 meter) height. Stairs and other service functions are secluded to the sides of each floor to provide maximum program space.

URBANUS

Taking its name from the Latin for city dweller, Urbanus Architecture & Design is unapologetic about its preoccupation with the contemporary metropolis. Developing strategies of urban infill that take particular note of the diversity of material conditions present in China's cities, the practice's methodology is girded by an earnest belief in the progressive mission of architecture and the utility of good design. This critical engagement is typified by a long-term study on the demographic effects of rapid urbanization, resulting in a recent monograph on the unique and often tenuous state of post-agrarian communities in populous Guangdong Province.

Liu Xiaodu, Meng Yan and Wang Hui founded Urbanus in 1999. With offices in Shenzhen and Beijing, the multidisciplinary firm has a portfolio spread over the map of the People's Republic, ranging from comprehensive urban master plans to interior design. Projects in development or under construction include Digital Beijing, on the Olympic Green (2007); a museum for the city of Tangshan, in Hebei Province (2007); the Nanyou Shopping Park (2007); and the Public Art Plaza (2006), both in Shenzhen.

All three founding principals of Urbanus were awarded their bachelors degrees in architecture from Tsinghua University in Beijing, where Meng and Wang both also received masters degrees. The trio received masters degrees in architecture from Miami University in Oxford, Ohio, and gained extensive professional experience in the United States.

OPPOSITE, LEFT TO RIGHT: *Meng Yan, Liu Xiaodu and Wang Hui.*

Urbanus
Beijing, 2005

OVERSEAS CHINESE TOWN
LIFE ART PLACE

Established in 1985 as a two-square-mile (5 km²) development zone overlooking Shenzhen Bay, the eponymous public corporation set up to run Overseas Chinese Town (OCT) is now a major developer with a significant national footprint. Known far and wide for building Vegas-like theme parks with names like "Splendid China" and "Happy Village," the company has also cultivated a quirky reputation for bundling residential master plans with its touristic spectacles. True to form, one of OCT's major housing developments, in the Chaoyang District of Beijing, is located in close proximity to a theme park it operates.

Urbanus was invited to design the sales office, and during the concept and design phases, the architects persuaded the client to make the 19,400-square-foot (1,800 m²) building into a cultural as well as a commercial operation. This exit strategy ultimately proved successful once the homes were all sold off, and OCT Life Art Place has since held a number of contemporary art exhibitions.

The basic composition is a glass box mounted over a podium. The floating box is a gallery space that offers a panoramic view of the park and the residential subdivision. The podium elevation facing the park to the east is open in its entirety, with the surrounding verdant patches also experienced as the backdrop for the interior. In contrast, a pair of concrete walls encloses the façade along a busy street, creating a retreat from the traffic noise.

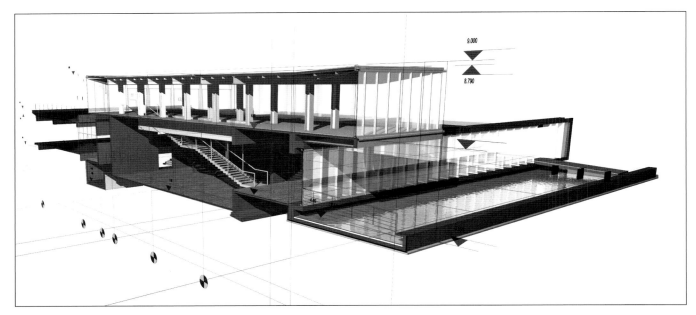

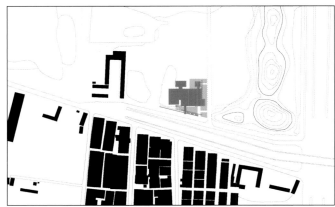

CLOCKWISE FROM LOWER LEFT: *Model, northeast view; model, southeast view; axonometric section looking north; site plan; pavilion view.*

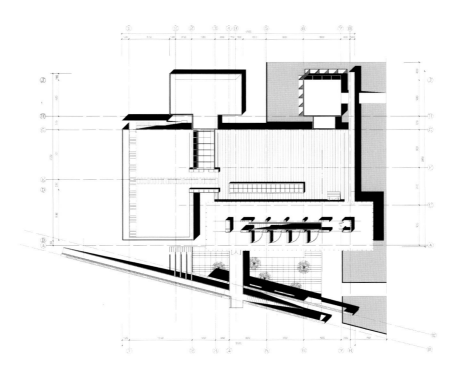

Second floor plan

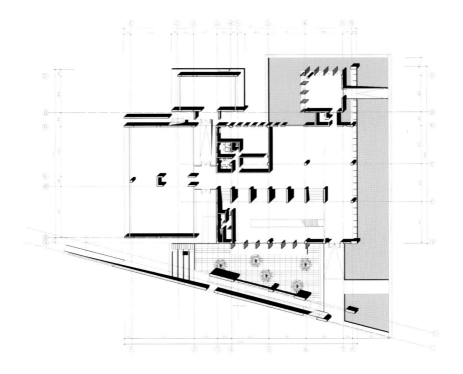

Ground floor plan

229

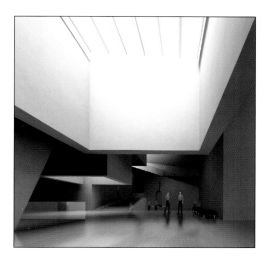

Urbanus
Shenzhen, Guangdong Province, Estimated Completion 2007

DAFEN ART MUSEUM

Once merely an appendage of greater Hong Kong, the growth of Shenzhen is often cast as the representative fable of "Opening and Reform," and the subsequent growth of its urban fabric an embodiment of the myriad complexities brought about by an extemporized approach to the planning of cities. Shenzhen's teeming districts present salient examples of "villages in the city," an ironic urban condition in which the ancient homes of peasants remain in place even as multilevel buildings consume the surrounding farmland.

The village of Dafen was at one time exclusively agrarian, but with Shenzhen's population ballooning from thirty thousand to ten million in less than three decades, the rapidly evolving demands of city life necessitated new vocations. One unique and reasonably sustainable model chosen by people here was the "painter's village." But unlike their high-art counterparts in Beijing, Dafenites chose to exploit a market for relatively cheap facsimiles of Old Master paintings and the like, chiefly to feed the growing appetite of the new middle classes for strictly decorative art—with many pieces retailing at Wal-Mart.

This 183,000-square-foot (17,000 m²) museum by Urbanus is a response to a very unusual program-matic dilemma. A conventional art museum would be considered out of place in the context of Dafen's peculiar urban culture. The question is whether the village could in time become a breeding ground for contemporary art. Therefore, the aspirational design strategy was to create a hybridized mix of different programs, with museum, studios, rental workshops, oil painting shops, and other commercial uses under one roof. The circulation plan fosters maximum interaction among its end users by creating several pathways through the building's public spaces, and programmatically linking it to the larger neighborhood.

The museum is sandwiched between commercial and other public programs, which intentionally allow for visual and spatial interactions among different functions. Exhibition, trade, painting and residence can happen simultaneously, threading through each other to weave a whole new urban web of interdependent relationships.

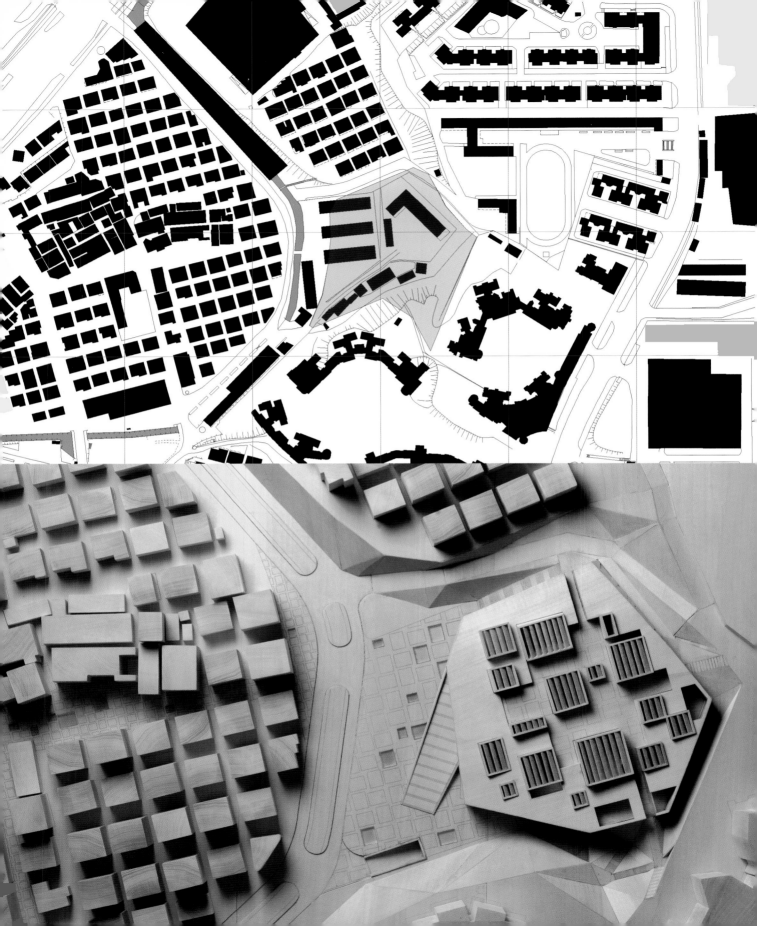

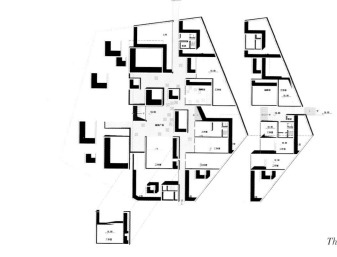

Third floor plan

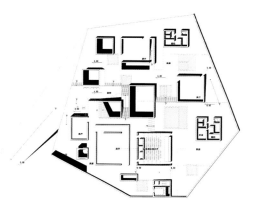

Second floor plan

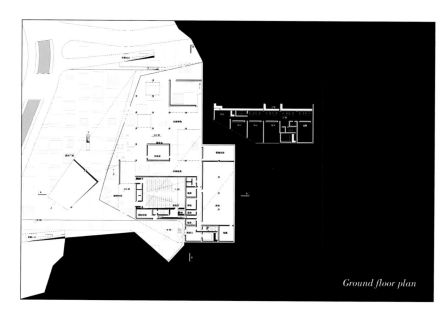

Ground floor plan

TOP LEFT: *Site plan: existing conditions*
BOTTOM LEFT: *Site model: full build-out*

Perspective renderings of potential exhibition programs

Urbanus
Shenzhen, Guangdong Province, 2004

OCAT

The existing site contains ten factory, warehouse, and dormitory buildings built in the early 1980s. Sandwiched between a growing middle-class residential area and a Disneyland manqué, this industrial node had by the turn of the century long lost its original purpose, and in 2003, Hexiangning Fine Arts Museum, one of the leading institutions of its kind in China, decided to set up a center for contemporary art in one of the warehouses. This decision coupled with the developer's intention to gradually transform this area into a hip, mixed-use district, with OCAT as the nucleus for the entire master plan.

The development strategy was a collaborative process between museum, developer, architect, and the artists and curators. The resulting plan was to simulate the natural growth of the city, starting from the linear-shaped addition to the existing warehouse, which will accommodate the new art center. Its name, OCAT, stands for OCT Contemporary Art Terminal—OCT being the acronym of Overseas Chinese Town, the developer.

The gaps between the buildings on the site are to be gradually filled up with other galleries, bookshops, cafés, bars, artist studios and design shops—along with a provision for lofts and apartments. In creating an interdependent set of uses, the master plan does not define a clear boundary, but instead attempts to set up a dynamic, interactive and flexible framework that can easily adapt to the new conditions posed by the accelerated transformation of the neighborhood and its adjacencies.

The shed housing the main exhibition program is transformed by wrapping the entire structure with framed metal mesh, an inexpensive and readily available industrial product with a transparency that leaves traces of the building's former life in view. In addition, the cavity between the wall and this new skin playfully disguises mechanical and building service functions.

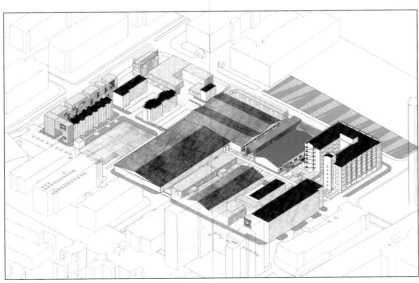

Axonometric site plan

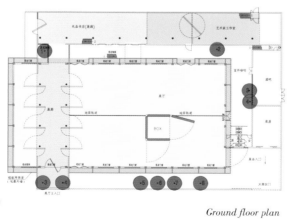

Ground floor plan

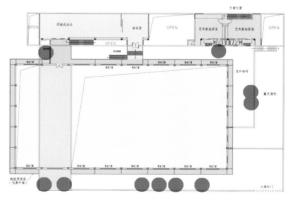

Second floor plan

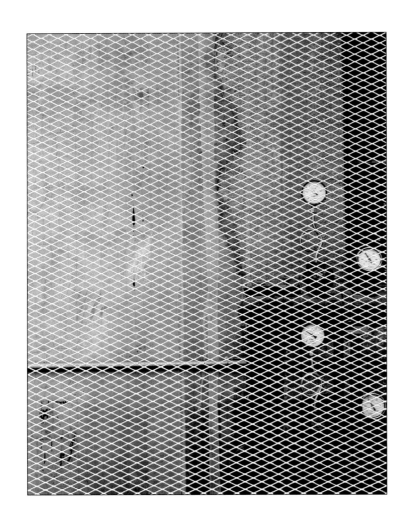

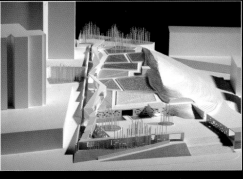

Model view looking north and looking south.

Urbanus
Shenzhen, Guangdong Province, Design Completed 2005

JADE BAMBOO

Prior to the onslaught of urban development in the early 1980s, the land on which Shenzhen sits was more or less hilly terrain. Most of the hills have been laid low, and the original topography is now hardly visible. Jade Bamboo Park is one of the few sites in the city center where the original landscape and flora stubbornly persist. It is a 111-acre (45 hectare) area embedded within the dense Luohu District—the first of Shenzhen's neighborhoods to be developed. At present, the park is not frequented by the general public due to limited access from its surrounding streets.

Adjacent to the north boundary of the park, and squeezed between upscale housing to the east and a cigarette factory to the west, a 65,000-square-foot (6000 m²) empty lot has the greatest potential for opening up another park entrance to the quiet residential street to the north. The property actually belongs to a neighboring residential tower block, but according to the zoning regulations it can only be used as a park with no commercial structures or housing. After protracted negotiations between the city and the developer of the apartment complex, the latter agreed to yield the right of use of the lot for an open public space connected to the planned new gate of Jade Bamboo Park. The understanding was that this effort would benefit both the residents of the housing development and the general public. As an emollient to the developer, the city agreed to build fifty parking spaces under the public plaza.

The site is an irregular trapezoid, which slopes up more than 43 feet (13 meters) from north to south. After close investigation of the site, Urbanus strongly recommended that the initial plan for a paved square, a large fountain, and especially a driveway up the hill be rethought in order to preserve the remaining hillside, existing vegetation and an old tomb behind the hill. Urbanus instead proposed three main elements on the site: first, a public cultural plaza adjacent to the street to the north with parking underneath; second, a winding corridor along the wall connecting the plaza below and the new park gate up the hill; and third, a series of terraced plantings between the remaining hill and the existing wall.

ILLUSTRATION CREDITS

ACKNOWLEDGMENTS

I would first like to express my gratitude to all the architects, whose innovative work gave vision and form to this book. In particular, I appreciate the valuable insight I received from Ai Weiwei, Wang Hui, Xu Tiantian, Zhang Lei, Rocco Yim, Gary Chang and especially, Yung Ho Chang and Sze Tsung Leong.

As ever, I am indebted to the editorial staff at Rizzoli International Publications in New York especially to publisher Charles Miers, senior architecture editor David Morton, and managing editor Ellen Nidy, for their continued patronage and friendship. Special thanks go to Dung Ngo, whose advice and powers of persuasion were much appreciated. I would also like to commend the following people for their professional support and their unending reservoirs of patience: Maria Pia Gramaglia, Kaija Markoe, Julie Schumacher, Colin G. Hough Trapp, Jerry Hoffnagle, Klaus Kirschbaum, Gloria Ahn, Pam Sommers, Julie di Filippo, Douglas Curran, Anet Sirna-Bruder, Jacquie Poirer, Paul Alwill, Alan Rutsky, Paul Richards, Joshua Machat, Meg Nolan, Jenny Lancaster, Linda Pricci and Jennifer Pierson.

The critical guidance and support I received from people across thee continents was likewise invaluable, particularly from Josh D. Jones, Eric Höweler, Mia Khimm, Andrea Hauge, Takatomo Kashiwabara, Kenichiro Suzuki, Edward Ng, David Leventhal, Kam Lee, Abner Castelo, Munenori Saito and Ricardo Cuerva. Special thanks go to Anna De Souza and Lauren Gould at Workhouse Publicity, and Chip Kidd at Alfred A. Knopf. I wish to also extend my gratitude to Toshiko Mori, whose timely and ever-decisive intercession propelled this endeavor forward.

Lastly, This anthology would not exist were it not for the material and moral contribution of Thomas Tsang and Eugene Lee. I cannot thank them enough for their untold hours of work, good humor and tenacious, can-do enthusiasm.

Ian Luna